Michaela Budiman

Contemporary Funeral Rituals of Sa'dan Toraja

From Aluk Todolo

to "New" Religions

CHARLES UNIVERSITY IN PRAGUE
KAROLINUM PRESS 2013

Reviewed by: Ing. Mgr. Zorica Dubovská (Prague)
Prof. Rudolf Mrázek, Ph.D. (Michigan)
PhDr. Tomáš Petrů, Ph.D. (Prague)

ISBN 978-80-246-2228-6

To my parents

Contents

Tidak ada agama yang saya benci, semua agama baik, sepanjang mereka itu mengejar kebenaran.

There is no religion that I do not respect; all religions are good if their quest is the pursuit of truth.

Tato' Dena'

Acknowledgements

This work was possible thanks to the selfless help of several people. However, whatever mistakes appear are mine alone. Firstly I would like to express my gratitude to my supervisor, Dr. Alena Oberfalzerová, for her consultancy, kindness and the time she dedicated to my intellectual pursuits. I wish to thank my teacher, Ing. Mgr. Zorica Dubovská, who motivated me to follow a more profound study of Indonesia, and who also inspired me to love this wonderful country. My deep gratitude goes to my family for supporting me both materially and emotionally throughout my studies at the university. In particular, I would like to thank my mother, Dr. Katarína Rybková, for her assistance with the final proofs of the present text, and my husband, Erik Herlambang Satrio Budiman, for his help with the transcription and analysis of the interviews I recorded in Indonesia. I would also like to thank my friends, Mgr. Ivan Hartmann, for editing the work in Czech and Karen McIntyre, for proofreading the English text. I am also deeply grateful to many other friends for the support they offered, as well as for their assistance with the final adjustments.

Naturally, the present work could not have materialized without the contribution of hundreds of Indonesians, and the Toraja in particular, whom I met during my field research, and who have helped me in countless ways. My gratitude goes to my main informant, Tato' Dena', an exceptional figure, who was willing to share with me part of his store of priceless knowledge regarding Toraja culture, and whose general approach to life provided a lesson in its own right and enriched me in human terms. Another key figure was the Catholic Priest, Drs. Lucas Paliling, LicIC. Apart from being a vital source of information, he provided me with a moral base to fall back on during my sojourn in Indonesia. Among the other people to whom I am indebted for advice are the Catholic priests, Drs. Stanislaus A. Dammen, MPS, MA. and Drs. Yohanes Manta' Rumengan. Additionally, I would like to thank the family of Stanislaus Dammen for their kindness and hospitality. I also wish to thank Drs. Paulus Palondongan, MM and Paulus Pasang Kanan, a number of relatives of Father Lucas, STIKPAR students, Mrs. Lily and other Toraja, whom for obvious reasons I cannot list here in entirety.

Kurre sumanga'!

1 Introduction

1.1 Themes and Objective of the Present Work

The present work discusses the Toraja ethnic group, who inhabit the Indonesian island of Sulawesi, and who, until the arrival of the first Dutch missionaries at the beginning of the 20th century, had essentially been cut off from the rest of the world. It can thus be said that until that point, the Toraja represented an isolated socio-cultural system. The present work draws on the field research of the author, which focused on the study of the most important contemporary Toraja ritual – the funeral – and furthermore on identifying and documenting the changes that have affected Toraja society as a result of their embrace of Christianity during the past century. The Toraja region, which is at present populated by the adherents of various Christian denominations, Islam, and the autochthonous religion *Aluk Todolo* (lit. the religion of the ancestors), offered an exceptionally rich and varied source material for study. The result of this field research is the present work, which aims to analyse the material gathered and to present a description of the formal and principal shifts expressed in the traditional rituals, which reflect seminal changes in terms of the role of religion. The book points out how Christianity, which has been adopted relatively recently, is incorporated into the indigenous religion and the customary law *adat*, which is derived from it. The present work ventures to explain why in less than a hundred years, almost 90 % of the population converted from *Aluk Todolo*, mainly to Christianity, also describing the process of conversion, and the extent to which (and in which localities) the new religion most visibly affected the form of modern-day rituals. The opinions of both Christians and minority adherents of *Aluk Todolo* are noted, especially with regard to the current situation, where funeral rites in particular represent a curious syncretic phenomenon, reflecting the societal changes that have taken place.

The body of textual, oral and audio-visual documentation collected by the author is unique, chiefly in that it includes interviews with one of the last living experts on the traditional Toraja religion. The present work offers the first processing of the material thus gathered, which is now ready for further expert review. It can be used for instance for linguistic analysis, or as a study from the perspective of the ethnography of communication, or in comparison with other ethnicities undergoing similar changes.

1.2   Structure of the Present Work

The present work is divided into two parts, logically interconnected, and sub-divided into chapters. The results of the research are summarized in the *Conclusion*.

The first part, *The Foundations of Toraja Culture*, is subdivided into three chapters surveying various aspects of Toraja culture. Chapter One, entitled *Tana Toraja and Its Inhabitants*, outlines the origin of the Toraja, as well as the etymology of the term *Toraja* itself. Given the cultural differences as well as the geographical remoteness of the country, it also presents brief essential information on the geography, climate and economic situation of the region. This is followed by an introduction into the Toraja language and available literature on the Toraja language and cultural traditions; the chapter closes by citing the historical milestones of the Toraja ethnic group. Chapter Two, *Autochthonous Religion* Aluk Todolo *and Adoption of Christianity,* presents the two main theories regarding the status of God, *Puang Matua,* in the indigenous religion. Another section is dedicated to the arrival of Protestant missionaries to the territory of present-day Toraja region, the foundation of the first schools, the arrival of Catholics in the area and the disputes of the two denominations which were sparked by their efforts to gain as many converts as possible. The final chapter of this part, *Important Aspects of Toraja Culture*, discusses the social stratification which – though officially abolished – is still evident in practice, and which even today to some extent determines the form of rituals. This is followed by a general classification of Toraja rituals and the classification of funeral rites based on the social status of the deceased. The chapter closes with the description of traditional Toraja houses, which play a crucial role during the rituals, and also of the burial chambers which form an integral pairing with the house, as well as the role of buffaloes, an essential fixture in most Toraja funerals.

The core of the work is presented in the second part of the book, entitled *Forms of Funeral Rituals in the Past and Today*, which is based almost exclusively on my own field research. The first chapter *General Information on Funeral Rites* outlines what happens to the soul of the deceased according to the indigenous Toraja belief, the ways in which the family of the deceased administers to the body, and the extent to which the social status and financial situation of the family influence the form and duration of this most important Toraja ritual in the present day. Next is a general outline of the funeral site and the accompanying rituals. The following chapter *The Actual Catholic Funeral and the Shift in Meaning in Some Rites Practised by Christians* describes the funeral of Yohana Maria Sumbung. The second part of this chapter is dedicated to the differences between funerals held in keeping with the rules of the indigenous religion, *Aluk Todolo*, and the contemporary Toraja rituals of Catholics and Protestants. The last two chapters, *Toraja Pentecostalists and Their Funerals* and *Toraja Muslims,* present interviews with adherents of both Pentecostalism and Islam, discussing the manner in which other religions have come to terms with Toraja traditions.

The *Conclusion* presents all the facts gleaned, particularly those gathered on the basis of field research. Appendices include the transcription of the interviews in the original Indonesian language, a list of the most important informants with brief biographical data, a timetable of the funeral of Yohana Maria Sumbung, the genealogy of the Gods nos. 1–3, an index and a glossary of Toraja and Indonesian terms used in the work, and a selection of photographs.

1.3 Research Thus Far

Given the fact that up until the beginning of the 20th century the Toraja ethnic group lacked a written tradition, researchers struggle with the absence of literature on Toraja history before this period. Therefore it is necessary to glean information about Toraja life only from myths, a far cry from modern-day historiography, or from the chronicles of the neighbouring ethnic group of the Bugis, most of which have been published and studied only in part. The first European to mention the modern Toraja was the Jesuit Father Gervaise, at the end of the 17th century.[1] The information he offers, however, does not originate

---

1   Nicolas Gervaise (1662–1729) was active in Siam (today Thailand) in the years 1681–1685. He was a Jesuit priest, a missionary, and eventually a bishop.

in personal experience, as it is merely drawn from his conversations with two Makassar princes who were students at the Jesuit College in Paris.[2]

From the 1920s onwards, various myths, folk tales, genealogies, songs, rhymes and proverbs were recorded and published, and there also emerged numerous works on linguistics. The first authors in the latter field were the Dutch, and in later years their place was taken by Toraja researchers. Available literature on Toraja history is relatively limited. The more ancient history is presented in a book by the Toraja author L. T. Tangdilintin *Toraja dan Kebudayaannya* [The Toraja and Their Culture]. Modern history dealing with events from 1860 until almost the end of the 20th century is laid out brilliantly in Terance Bigalke's (US) work *Tana Toraja: A Social History of an Indonesian People*.[3] The Dutch scholar Hetty Nooy-Palm in her two books *The Sa'dan-Toraja: A Study of Their Social Life and Religion I. Organization, Symbols and Beliefs* (1979) and *The Sa'dan-Toraja: A Study of Their Social Life and Religion II: Rituals of the East and West* (1986) provides a detailed description of traditional Toraja culture and its rituals in their original form, before the arrival of Christianity. Another influential book on Toraja culture and, in particular, funerals is *Feasts of Honor: Ritual and Change in the Toraja Highlands* (1985) by Toby Alice Volkman. Apart from the above-cited works, there are a number of other publications concerned chiefly with the traditional form of Toraja rituals. A book dealing with the changes that Toraja society underwent in the last decades – *Paths and Rivers: Sa'dan Toraja Society in Transformation* – was published in 2009 by Roxana Waterson, who has studied the Toraja since 1978. The present work, however, does not draw on Waterson's findings, as my dissertation in Czech, on which the present English translation is based, had been defended one year previously, in 2008. Although the present work is based above all on my field research, the information cited in the part *The Foundations of Toraja Culture* is drawn from the above-mentioned specialized literature.

1.4   Field Research and Methods of Work

The material on which the present work draws is the result of two field research expeditions I undertook in the Toraja region, on the island of Sulawesi. The first of those took place between mid-February and mid-March of 2002,[4] and its chief

---

2 *Nooy-Palm* 1979, pp. 8–9.
3 This book was only published in 2005, nonetheless it is Bigalke's hitherto unpublished 1982 dissertation entitled *A Social History of "Tana Toraja" 1870–1965*.
4 After receiving an Indonesian Government scholarship, I spent the academic year 2001–2002 at the prestigious Universitas Gajah Mada in Java, in the city of Yogyakarta. During the second semester I went to Sulawesi in order to gather the necessary study material for my diploma work.

benefit was becoming acquainted with the socio-cultural environment of the region. The second six-month-long field research undertaken in 2005–2006 was more systematic in nature, underpinned both by deeper personal knowledge and significantly better technical support.

Like many others, I struggled with a variety of problems during my field research. In spite of my fairly good knowledge of the environment, it was far from easy to constantly keep in mind all the rules and codes of social life which determine the everyday affairs of the Toraja in a fundamental way. Another delicate task was making the video recordings of the rituals – often, this constituted balancing on the verge between public space and the intimate sphere of the people involved. My primary aim was to gather as much material, video recordings and information as possible without committing a faux pas which would block my access to the community I was observing. On the other hand, my sojourn in the Toraja region was facilitated by the fact that Indonesians in general are highly friendly to foreigners. Most felt honoured by the presence of a European woman at their rituals, and as a result, I generally met with a positive reception.[5] Working with people who have recently lost someone dear to them, however, was rather demanding psychologically, presenting frequent dilemmas regarding how to articulate my queries as sensitively as possible so as not to hurt or offend the bereaved, and at the same time, to gather the necessary information.

Throughout my field research, I lived at the invitation of my informant, Priest Lucas Paliling, whom I had met already during my first sojourn there, in the city of Rantepao at a building belonging to the STIKPAR school,[6] which he had founded and where he served as director.[7] From Rantepao I made regular excursions to the nearby surroundings, where I participated in funerals. Among the field research methods I applied were participant observation and interview. Wherever possible, I would prepare at least a general field of questions, which I would then utilise freely. I deliberately avoided structured question and answer sessions, since given the nature of the environment, they would be very artificial and the replies of my respondents would lose their immediacy.

After the conclusion of the rites at which I was present, I would review the recordings I took as well as the photo-documentation, preparing questions to then put to a selected informant from the family hosting the given ritual.

---

5   Throughout my sojourn, I tried not to stand out too much. I thus strove to dress, eat and communicate as the Toraja do.

6   STIKPAR (Sekolah Tinggi Kateketik dan Pastoral) – Rantepao Catechetic and Pastoral Institute.

7   Before his tenure in Rantepao, he held the office of the rector of the Universitas Atma Jaya in Makassar.

Several days after the ceremony itself, I would meet the person I had selected as my informant and record the ensuing interview, which as a rule would be semi-structured. I would then analyse these materials after my return from my field research. The present work offers an intersection of ethnological and psychological perspectives. It describes the impact of the conversion to new religions on Toraja people.

1.5   Informants

I list all of my major informants and their basic data in an appendix entitled *Main Informants*. Here I shall mention two of my key sources in more detail.

My main informant was Tato' Dena', from the village of Mandetek in the Tallulembangna region,[8] and an adherent of the autochthonous religion *Aluk Todolo* who performs the priestly roles of *tominaa* and *tomenani*.[9] Tato' Dena' only enrolled in school at the age of thirteen, and until then – according to Toraja tradition – he had tended buffaloes. His formal education lasted eight years (six years of grammar school and two years of junior secondary school). Already at a young age (and despite being the youngest of all his siblings) his father, who likewise performed these sacred functions, chose him to be his successor, and over time, he passed on to him the great store of his knowledge.

My interviews with this wise man, which amounted to a unique eighteen-hour long recording, exerted a seminal influence on the form of the present work. At the moment, there exists no other person who knows more about traditional Toraja culture and indigenous religion in the Tallulembangna region than my main informant.[10] In one interview he himself expressly cited: "When I am gone from Tallulembang, from Mandetek (*when I die*), there will certainly no longer remain another who knows the rules."[11] It is obvious from his testimony that

---

8   Southern part of the Toraja region.
9   See chapt. 1.2.2.
10 I know from Tato' Dena's account that he formerly provided information to several anthropologists researching the indigenous customs and religion of the Toraja. In 2007 Roxana Waterson (Associate Professor in the Department of Sociology at the National University of Singapore) made a documentary film about Tato' Dena' entitled *When the Sun Rises: A Toraja Priest of the Ancestral Way*. In the year 2009 she published the book *Paths and Rivers: Sa'dan Toraja Society in Transformation* where she presents much of the information provided to her by Tato' Dena'. There were also Eric Crystal (retired at present, with over thirty years of close study of Southeast Asia, including lecturing at the University of California, Berkley and at the San Francisco Art Institute) and Dimitri Tsintjilonis (lecturer in social anthropology at the University of Edinburgh, focusing chiefly on the phenomenon of death, religion and ritual in Indonesia and Southeast Asia). He also gave interviews to the ethnomusicologist Dana Rappoport, who wrote a dissertation on Toraja music.
11 Mandetek is a village in the region of Tallulembang.

he regards himself as the last living person versed in the traditions, at least in the region where he lives. In our interviews he exuded composure and spiritual serenity resulting from his faith in God and his belief that throughout his life he has acted righteously, observing the rules set by the ancestors and mediating communication with Divinity for his people. With an admirable equanimity, he accepted life in all its forms, speaking with understanding and tolerance about individuals whom others would consider rivals or even enemies. At times he illustrated his deliberate and systematic discourse by means of bamboo sticks.[12] He categorically refused to discuss matters where he was – in his opinion – insufficiently informed (e.g. life after death, the distribution of meat at funerals, or polygyny). His opinions and behaviour manifested the great importance he attached to living in harmony with God, nature, family and the rest of humanity. Given the fact that *Aluk Todolo* is a religion on the verge of real extinction, to the uninitiated, Tato' Dena's attitude towards passing his extraordinary knowledge on to the next generations may appear surprisingly passive. This attitude, however, is based on the belief that his successor will be designated by God. As that has not happened so far, he largely keeps his knowledge to himself, and, as can be seen from the above quote, he is reconciled even to the eventuality that he might not have a successor.

A diametrically opposite view on Toraja culture was offered to me by another major informant, the Catholic Priest Lucas Paliling. He is a university-educated man, whose two-year long studies in Rome and several other trips to Europe made him rather well acquainted with European traditions and their general way of life. His great contribution lay in his ability to look at Toraja culture simultaneously from the perspective of a member of this ethnicity and from the vantage point of a scholar used to living in a different environment. Apart from being an invaluable source of vital information, I am also indebted to him for providing me with a material basis and emotional support.

1.6   Gathered Material and Methods of Analysis

In the course of my research I gathered over forty-five hours of audio and twenty-two hours of video recordings and hundreds of photographs. After returning from my field research, I listened to all the recordings, noting the most important information. In some cases, my analysis concluded that their value as testimony was so exceptional that I decided to transcribe, translate, and furnish

---

12 These are about 15 cm long and 0.5 cm thick bamboo stalks used by the Toraja as illustrative tools when providing explanations.

them with explanatory comments. I believe that the literal transcription of my interviews provides a more vivid picture of Toraja culture from the perspective of the Toraja themselves. The manner in which these informants speak, as well as the fact that at times they duplicate the presented information, while at other times avoiding the description of certain phenomena, their choice of terms or turns of phrase, similes or metaphor, are all highly telling. For this reason, I incorporated in this work a number of literal transcriptions of interviews translated into English (as well as citing them in the original Indonesian), so they may be used for further review.

In analysing some interviews I encountered a number of linguistic problems, resulting mainly from the fact that Indonesian is not the mother tongue of the Toraja.[13] Understanding was often rather difficult, due to the mistaken use of some words and unorthodox word order. I analysed problematic passages with the help of a native speaker of Indonesian.

In most cases, the interviews were translated more loosely for the sake of better understanding; however, where the informant used a curious turn of phrase, I cite these expressions in literal translation, with a loose translation following in italics in brackets in English. In some cases, the text features an English word (in italics and in brackets) which the informant did not actually use, but which nonetheless clarifies the utterance. Where Toraja terms are left in the text, they are followed by an explanation in brackets (without italics), and where these are translated; literal translations are indicated by the abbreviation "lit.". For the sake of clarity, the interviews are often commented on directly in the text. All interviews transcribed verbatim are cited in the appendix in Indonesian.

The appendix *Photographs* features images representing Toraja culture – starting with houses and burial chambers and then moving on to pictures of funeral rites, closing with portraits of individuals.

Bibliographical Note

This work is based on the first half of my Ph.D. thesis, which I successfully defended in the year 2008. Some parts of the work have previously appeared in published articles (see Bibliography).

---

13 The native tongue of almost all Indonesians is the language spoken in a given locality, in this case Toraja. Indonesian (a standardized dialect of Malay, used as a lingua franca in the region for several centuries) was declared the official language of Indonesia in 1945. However, Indonesian is the mother tongue of only a very small percentage of Indonesians. Most of the population only learn it at school.

The Indonesian Alphabet and Sounds

Throughout the present work, I have used the orthography codified and in effect in Indonesia and Malaysia as of 1972. It is essentially a phonetic orthography.

The Alphabet[14]

First I give the letter, and then an approximation of the pronunciation of its name.

a – *ah*, but short. It has the sound of "a" in English "Ha!".
b – *bé*
c – *ché*. Has the sound of English "ch".
d – *dé*
e – *é*. There are two quite distinct sounds written with this letter.
(a) The first is a "mute" or unstressed "e" sound (called schwa), as in English "delight", where we could insert an apostrophe: "ragg'd".
(b) The second is less common, and like the familiar "e" of English "met". In normal Indonesian writing, the two kinds of "e" are not distinguished, but luckily, the dictionaries help us by marking this second "e" with an acute accent (é).
f – *ef*
g – *gé*. Has the sound of "g" in English "get".
h – *ha*
i – *ee*, but short. Has the sound of "i" in English "in".
j – *jé*
k – *kah*, but short. Like in English, except that in final position it is "unreleased" (glottal stop).
l – *el*
m – *em*
n – *en*
o – *oh*. Has the sound of "o" in English "hot".
p – *pé*
q – *kee,* but short.
r – *air*. This letter is always sounded, no matter where it occurs. It is the lightly rolled "r", not the American "r" or the guttural "r" of French or German, in any position.
s – *ess*
t – *té*

---

14 *Robson* 2010, pp. xiii–xvii.

u – *oo*. Has the sound of "u" in English "put".
v – *fé*
w – *wé*
x – *iks*
y – *yé*
z – *zet*

Other Consonants:
kh – has the sound of "ch" of Scottish "loch"
sy – has the sound of English "sh"

Genuine Diphthongs:
au – has the sound of "ow" in English "down"
ia – has the sound of "i" in English "like"
oi – has the sound of "oy" in English "boy"

The Toraja Alphabet and Sounds
The pronunciation of the Toraja language is the same as Indonesian. However, some of the graphemes do not exist in the Toraja language (c, f, v, x, z). On the other hand it is very common in Toraja that, unlike in Indonesian, letters are doubled (e.g. r, k, l,). The Toraja language also distinguishes itself with its utilization of the glottal stop, which is indicated in the text by an apostrophe (e.g. Sa'dan).

Abbreviations:
Ind. = Indonesian
Gk. = Greek
lit. = literally
Sa. = Sanskrit
Tor. = Toraja

2   The Foundations
of Toraja Culture

2.1   Overview

The aim of the first part of the present work is to provide an introduction
to the Toraja ethnic group as well as to the key aspects of their culture. The
chapter entitled *Tana Toraja and Its Inhabitants* discusses the given region and its
geography, climate and economy, the Toraja themselves and the etymology of
the ethnonym *Toraja*. The next chapter, *The Autochthonous Religion* Aluk Todolo
and the Adoption of Christianity deals with the nature of indigenous religious
beliefs and the arrival of Christianity in the Toraja region at the beginning of the
20th century. The last chapter entitled *Important Aspects of Toraja Culture* discusses
in particular social stratification, the classification of rituals, the important
role of traditional homes, the role of burial vaults and the buffalo, the most
important animal in Toraja culture.

2.2   Tana Toraja and Its Inhabitants

2.2.1 Origins of the Population

Anthropologists rank the Toraja, along with the Batak of Sumatra, and the
Dayak of Borneo, among the first wave of Proto-Malay migrations. The culture
of these three ethnic groups bears a notable similarity to the Dong Son culture,[15]

---

15   The Dong Son culture is a Bronze Age culture (7th century BC – 2nd century BC), named after
the Dong Son archaeological site in northern Vietnam. It is typified by the production of large

which has led scholars to conclude that the Toraja originate from Dong Son, An Nam, or Indochina.[16] The exact date of arrival is not known, nevertheless most sources cite the dating to the period between 3000–2000 BC. The Toraja brought the Stone and Iron Age culture with them.[17] They set out from Dong Son via two routes, with one group travelling south through Malaysia, Sumatra and Java, while the other group chose a route via China to Japan and the Philippines and from there south to Sulawesi, Borneo, and other islands of the Indonesian archipelago.[18] Around 300–200 BC the Toraja were pushed inland by the second migration wave of the Deutero-Malay people – who include peoples such as the Bugis and the Makassar, inhabiting the Sulawesi coast.

2.2.2 Contemporary Understanding of the Term Toraja and the Ethnological Classification of the Toraja

Cultural anthropology originally used the word Toraja as a generic term denoting the non-Muslim populations of Central and South Sulawesi.[19] At the beginning of the 20th century, the Dutch ethnographers and missionaries Nicholas Adriani and Albert C. Kruyt divided this population into three main groups: the East Toraja, also known as Poso-Tojo or Bare'e Toraja; West Toraja, also known as Palu-Koro or Parigi-Kaili Toraja; and South Toraja, also termed Tae' or Sa'dan Toraja.[20] At present, the first two groups inhabit the province of Central Sulawesi, while the South Toraja live in what is today the territory of South Sulawesi Province. There are considerable differences between these groups, particularly between the East and West Toraja on one hand, and the South Toraja on the other. The most pronounced differences can be seen in language,[21] religion, social stratification, traditional architecture, agriculture, and the techniques used in weaving, as well as in other areas. Anthropologists

---

bronze drums. It stretched to adjoining regions of South China, Cambodia, Laos, Malaysia and Indonesia. For a long time it was regarded as the most ancient culture in South-East Asia. Newer research, however, indicates that it in fact followed up on an older tradition reaching back as far as the turn of the 4th and 3rd millennia BC.

16 However, according to a different, more recent theory, the first wave emerged from Taiwan, continued to Phillipines, Sulawesi, Borneo and further to the south (*Munoz* 2006, pp. 29–30).

17 *Sandarupa* 2000, p. 11.

18 *Salombe'* 1972, p. 11.

19 Sulawesi (189 216 km², 16 million inhabitants) is the third largest island of Indonesia, and the eleventh largest worldwide (maps of Sulawesi and Indonesia – p. 40). It is surrounded by Borneo to the west, Flores and Timor to the south, the Maluku Islands to the east, and the Philippines in the north. Sulawesi consists of six provinces: Gorontalo, West Sulawesi, South Sulawesi, Central Sulawesi, South-Eastern Sulawesi, and Northern Sulawesi.

20 *Liku Ada'* 1986, p. 9.

21 *Nooy-Palm* 1975, p. 53.

who would later study the population of the mountain regions of South and Central Sulawesi eventually modified this earlier classification. An essential change was made by the American anthropologist and sociologist Raymond Kennedy, who eliminated distinctions between the Eastern and Western branches. Instead, he united them into a single group, which he called Toraja. To distinguish the members of the southern branch, he termed them Sa'dan. On the other hand, anthropologist Walter Kaudern, for instance, stressed that the Sa'dan have much in common with the rest of the Toraja.[22] Referring to the works of Adriani and Kruyt, the ethnologist Nooy-Palm cites that despite certain differences, the East, West and also South of Toraja display a number of shared cultural features. The buffaloes, for example, play a pivotal role in the culture of all of the Toraja, while another fact impossible to overlook is that some rituals are almost identical. Adriani also claims that the separate groups of the Toraja share very similar myths and stories featuring the same animals, particularly roosters and buffaloes,[23] as well as the notion of Upperworld and the World under the Earth.[24]

It is somewhat of an irony that both the Adriani and Kruyt classification, and subsequently the Kennedy modification, depart radically from contemporary usage – for the term Toraja never became current in the area of Central Sulawesi. On the contrary, it is used today exclusively to denote inhabitants of the Sa'dan territory.[25]

In the present work, however, which discusses the Sa'dan Toraja, I will use the single term Toraja.

2.2.3 Etymology of the Term Toraja

The term *Toraja* started to gain currency approximately during the 17th century, when the Toraja came into contact with other ethnic groups. Its etymology is not exactly known; however, there are a variety of hypotheses. According to one of these, the name *Toraja* comes from the Bugis language, and is made up of three words: *to-ri-aja. To* – man, *ri* – preposition "of", *aja* – the hinterland, or the preposition "above". *Toraja* thus denotes "people from the mountains", or "people from the hinterland". This is how the Bugis were said to have referred to their neighbours who had settled in the interior highland of Sulawesi. The name *Toraja* can be understood as being antonymous to the name *To*

---

22 *Liku Ada'* 1986, p. 10.
23 Both animals continue to have great importance for the Toraja.
24 *Nooy-Palm* 1975, p. 73.
25 *Bigalke* 2005, p. 7.

Luwu' – "people living by the sea"; *to* – man, and *luwu'* – sea (*luwu'* > *luu'* > *lu'* > *loo'* > *lau'* > *laut*).[26]

Nicholas Adriani and Albert C. Kruyt likewise believed [27] that the term is a compound of three words, but thought the last of those to mean north.[28] According to this theory, this was the name the Bugis gave to the Toraja as the latter inhabited an area to the north of their territory. Adriani and Kruyt were the first foreigners to borrow the ethnonym *Toraja* from the Bugis, applying it to the people living in the interior of Central Sulawesi and South Sulawesi.[29] Later this denomination was adopted by other scholars, Dutch government officials, and travellers as well as writers. According to another hypothesis, the expression *Toraja* originates in the Luwu' area inhabited by the Bugis, and is made up of two words: *to* – *rajang* – "people from the west"; for the Toraja settled the area west of Luwu'.[30]

Another theory cites the mythic figure of the Toraja prince Lakipada, who set on a quest for immortality and is said to have reached the Makassar Kingdom of Gowa most likely at some point in the late 13th century. The local people did not know from where he came, but based on various attributes they recognized him as a member of a royal family, whose noble origin was further attested also by the fact that he came from the east. According to local mythology, in South Sulawesi kings always came from the east. Lakipada was thus given the name *Tau Raya*, meaning "Man from the East" in the Makassar language. It was this name that was believed to have given rise to the term *Toraja*.[31]

The Toraja writer Marampa' cites [32] that today the Toraja call themselves *To Raa* or *Toraya*. *To Raa* is composed of two words, i.e. *to* – man, and *raa* – *generous*. The expression *Toraya* is also a compound of two words: *to* – man, and *raya* – great, thus *Toraya* denotes a man respected and revered.[33]

Leaving aside Toraja folk etymology, one may presume that the designation *Toraja* derives from the neighbouring ethnic groups. Several centuries ago this had a negative connotation, when the Bugis and the Makassar inhabiting the

---

26   *Salombe'* 1972, p. 7.
27   *Nooy-Palm* 1975, p. 54.
28   According to these ethnographers, in the Bugis language, *aja/raja* originally meant north; the equivalent term in Malaysian is *daya/dayak;* in Toraja it is *daa/daya* (*Nooy-Palm* 1975, p. 54).
29   *Salombe'* 1972, p. 7.
30   *Tangdilintin* 1975, p. 2.
31   *Tangdilintin* 1975, p. 3.
32   *Marampa'* (*Mengenal Toraja*), p. 31.
33   There also exists a notion, which I nonetheless regard as unlikely, according to which the word *Toraja* originally comes from the Sanskrit *raja* – king (in Indonesian the word *raja* also means king). According to this hypothesis, all Toraja would thus be descendants of a royal house. In the past, Toraja society was strongly stratified and this stratification is apparent even today (a theme I will discuss later), and for this reason the theory is received less than enthusiastically by the aristocracy. If all Toraja were to be regarded as of noble descent, then the aristocracy would naturally lose their exclusive status.

lowlands used it to denote the various peoples who lived in the highlands.[34] People in the Sa'dan highlands as well as the population scattered in the mountains of south and central Sulawesi did not use the term. The Sa'dan formerly used to be called after their native village – for example, *to Pao* was a person hailing from the Pao village.

The inhabitants of the Sa'dan highlands did not start to refer to themselves as *Toraja* until the 1920s and 1930s, when there occurred a gradual rise in ethnic awareness. The terms Tana Toraja and the Toraja should thus not be used in relation to events which occurred before the beginning of the 20th century, since this might create the false impression that there in fact existed some degree of solidarity and tribal unity between the groups inhabiting the Sa'dan highlands.[35] In reality this scenario could not be further from the truth, as village communities existed independently of each other, most likely uniting on only one solitary occasion – in the 17th century, when they confronted the Bugis leader Arung Palakka.[36] When discussing the period before the 20th century, I use the phrase Sa'dan highlands or mountain range instead of Tana Toraja, and the Sa'dan instead of the Toraja.[37]

2.2.4 Geography, Climate and Economy of the Toraja Region

In order to get a better idea of the Toraja way of life, it is necessary to provide a brief overview of the geography, climate and economy of the Toraja region, as well as citing some basic facts which are essential for understanding a culture rather different from the Western viewpoint.

Indonesia is formed by thirty-three provinces in total, which are further divided into administrative units – regencies (*kabupaten*). Until the year 2008, the Toraja occupied *kabupaten* Tana Toraja in the northern portion of the province of South Sulawesi. However, in that year the regency was divided into two separate parts:[38] Tana Toraja and Toraja Utara, thus at present the Toraja inhabit two *kabupatens*.[39] The southern border of the Tana Toraja *kabupaten* lies 310 km north of Makassar, the capital of the province of South Sulawesi.[40] The

---

34 *N'ha Sandra* 1998, p. 1.
35 *Bigalke* 2005, pp. 6–8.
36 *N'ha Sandra* 1998, p. 4.
37 I use this term to denote the inhabitants of the Sa'dan highlands, who share roughly the same language, customs and religion, but not the sense of common ethnic identity.
38 The reasons for the separation are mentioned in section 2.4.1.
39 In this work, I will use the term "Toraja region" for the two regencies: Tana Toraja and Toraja Utara.
40 South of this *kabupaten* there lie the *kabupatens* of Enrekang and Pinrang, to the north-east there is Luwu', to the north Mamuju, and to the west Polewali Mamasa.

total area of these two regencies is 3,205 km². The Toraja region is an extremely mountainous territory, with mountains making up 40% of the total area.[41] Through the area flows the Sa'dan River, the longest watercourse in Southern Sulawesi. It is from this river that the local population takes its name. From October to June there begins the dry season, with minimal precipitation; in the rainy season from December to April, it rains for several hours practically every day. May and November are interim months. According to the census undertaken in 2004 the Tana Toraja and Toraja Utara *kabupatens* together have a total of 429,859 inhabitants.[42] More than a million Toraja have settled in other regions of Indonesia. The capital and simultaneously the administrative centre of Tana Toraja is Makale. Rantepao, which is located near all of the main tourist landmarks, has thus become a hub of tourism and local culture, as well as trade. It is the capital of the newly-formed Toraja Utara.

The main source of sustenance of the inhabitants of Tana Toraja is agriculture (approximately 90 % of the inhabitants are farmers), using both dry fields (*ladang*), and irrigated fields (*sawah*). The main staple crops are rice, coffee, ginger, cassava, cloves and vegetables. Rice, which is grown on irrigated terrace fields, is planted manually and harvested by plough, sometime driven by a buffalo. Unlike the exceptionally fertile region of Java, Tana Toraja typically has a harvest only once per year. The production of rice does not entirely cover local demand and it is thus partially imported from nearby areas. Locally, mainly in the *kecamatan*[43] Mengkendek, rice is harvested alternately with yields of potato or cabbage. These crops, including other vegetables (such as carrots or corn) are grown by Indonesian farmers chiefly in the mountains, from where they are exported to the lowlands. The main export article at present is coffee, grown in Tana Toraja roughly since the latter part of the 19th century, followed by cocoa, which is designated predominantly for the European market. The youngest crop grown here, popular with local farmers for its high sale prices, is vanilla, likewise exported to Europe. Due to the constant growth of the population, Tana Toraja suffers from a shortage of fertile land, in spite of ongoing cultivation of further mountainside areas. It is for this reason in particular that many Toraja have been leaving their homeland since the 1960s in search of work in other parts of Indonesia. Many of them have settled in Java, while others have found employment with mining or oil companies in Kalimantan and West Papua; some others have also left for Malaysia.

---

41 The mountains lie at an altitude of 1,500–3,083 m above sea level.
42 *Tana Toraja dalam Angka* (2004, p. 6). The title of the book uses only the term Tana Toraja, because when it was published the Toraja Utara regency did not yet exist – it was created in 2008 when the northern part of Tana Toraja gained independence.
43 *Kecamatan* is a territorial administrative unit. Several *kecamatan* compose a *kabupaten*.

In terms of livestock, the buffalo is regarded as the most important, playing as it does a unique role in Toraja culture, particularly in its funeral rites, while also providing a source of livelihood. Pigs are bred by the Toraja not only for their own use, but also for the non-Muslim section of the population living in nearby cities such as Makassar or Pare-Pare. Goat and horse breeding is rare, for the Toraja do not eat their meat. Poultry and fish, on the other hand, are highly popular. Fish are often stocked in the irrigated rice fields which happen to be momentarily free from crops, where they are caught with specially adjusted baskets.

As for crafts, fabric weaving has the longest tradition, but the Toraja nonetheless also smelt iron and copper to make agricultural tools, knives and axes. Woodcarving has become widespread at this point; however, it is not a traditional craft in the area. The Toraja have started carving scale models of their characteristic houses and small buffalo statuettes as well as other objects symbolizing their culture only in the latter half of the 20th century in response to the demands of the tourist industry. Commerce in Tana Toraja is conducted mainly at markets which are held regularly every six days; the most well-known are those in the cities of Rantepao and Makale. Every sixth day, a special market is held two kilometres north of Rantepao, where only buffaloes and pigs are traded.

Tourism provides another source of livelihood for the Toraja. This industry started to develop here only since the 1970s. Starting in the late 1960s,[44] the Indonesian government has undertaken an intensive effort to promote tourism across the whole of Indonesia, and in the years 1969–1973 they concentrated primarily on areas with good access for visitors, such as Java, the north of Sumatra and Bali. In the years that followed they focused on the other islands, among them Sulawesi. Part of the plan was to attract tourists to remote destinations whose development required financing that could be provided by tourism. The Toraja region was interesting in this respect particularly for its peculiar funeral rites and way of life, which Western travelers found archaic and therefore very attractive. The first tourists started to come to this area in the early 1970s, with their numbers continuing to grow each year.[45] Tana Toraja saw the

---

44   On September 30, 1965, there was a coup in Indonesia, with the result that the first Indonesian president Sukarno was deposed (1901–1970; in power 1945–1967) and replaced by general Suharto (1921–2008; in power 1967–1998), who totally changed the political orientation of the country, steering it towards the West. After a brutal putsch, in the course of which likely up to hundreds of thousands of sympathisers of the *PKI* (*Partai Komunis Indonesia* – Communist Party of Indonesia) were murdered, Suharto installed what is known as *Orde Baru* (New Order), the opposite of the *Orde Lama* (Old Order). Foreign capital started to trickle into Indonesia, and among other things, the government sought to support tourism which was to boost the development of the economy.

45   In 1971 the country started to keep statistics on the number of tourists in the region. 58 tourists visited Tana Toraja that year. Four years later the figure was already 6,008 persons (*Crystal* 1978, p. 111).

largest numbers of visitors in the late 1980s and early 1990s.[46] In 1996, however, Indonesia as a whole was swept by a wave of social unrest, and the numbers of tourists dropped dramatically as a result. In December 1996 ethnic clashes erupted in West Kalimantan, followed by a financial crisis attended by numerous demonstrations in major cities in July 1997.[47] On May 21, 1998, President Suharto resigned (the end of his era effectively ended the massive promotion of tourism), but the unrest continued. In May 1998, there were anti-Chinese rebellions, in January 1999 conflicts in Ambon, in May 2000 in the Poso region in Central Sulawesi, and subsequently in many other places. All of these events were well-reported by the international media and it is therefore hardly surprising that Indonesia at this point was not a sought-after tourist destination. The drop in the numbers of visitors was also strongly affected by subsequent fears of the radicalization of Islam, and the terrorist attacks on Bali in the years 2002 and 2005.[48] The least successful year in terms of tourism in Tana Toraja was 2004, which saw almost ten times fewer tourists than a decade before. One may therefore summarize that despite the rapid rise of tourism in the 1970s (which was mostly the result of a government program to promote Indonesia), the negative social events of the 1990s and early 21st century contributed to the fact that tourism failed to become to the Toraja a source of reliable income as expected, and most inhabitants continue to sustain themselves by agriculture.

2.2.5 Key Historical Events

2.2.5.1 Arrival of Javanese Merchants

As we know from oral tradition, in roughly the 15th century Javanese merchants arrived to the Sa'dan highlands from the south, selling various decorative objects, such as ceramics, batik cloths, and gold trinkets, which are kept among the scions of the local aristocracy to this day, and passed from one generation to the next. The most famous of these merchants was Puang Rade'.[49] Tradition

---

46 The high numbers of tourists visiting Tana Toraja in the first half of the 1990s were doubtless also the result of the promotion of the country by the "Visit Indonesia Year 1992" program. It was mostly under the administration of President Suharto that local governments received subsidies for the support and development of tourism. In 1994, 258,700 tourists visited Tana Toraja (*Adams* 1998, p. 81).

47 Experts believe that the economic crisis in Indonesia was part of the East Asian financial crisis, which in 1997 swept through South Korea, Thailand and Indonesia, and also partly affected Hong Kong, Malaysia, Laos and the Philippines.

48 Indonesia is the largest Muslim country in the world. Of the total population of approx. two hundred and thirty million (data of 2007) circa 86 % are Muslim.

49 It is likely that the name Rade' emerged as a corruption of the Javanese noble title Raden.

has it that together with the members of his retinue he taught the Sa'dan to work with gold, and to use it in the production of decorative objects – particularly ornaments for traditional daggers, the *gayang*. Their handles are often rendered in the form of a dragon, or display Hindu motifs.[50] The Javanese merchants also introduced elements of the Javanese culture, which at the time was Hindu, and in turn also influenced both local art and the form of government. Some of them married local women, settling here. Although in the end the Bugis traders from the surrounding kingdoms of Bone, Luwu' and Sidenreng forced the Javanese to leave the Sa'dan highlands, these still managed to leave traces in Toraja culture. The Bugis arrived to the Sa'dan Highlands at the beginning of the 17th century, having learned from the Javanese that the locals owned large amounts of gold and were willing to exchange it for ornaments and various finely woven fabrics of different colours.

2.2.5.2 The Bugis Under the Leadership of Arung Palakka

In 1675 the army of the respected and feared Bugis prince Arung Palakka occupied the Sa'dan Highlands. After the arrival of the Bugis, gambling with cards and dice became an inseparable part of local social life. Until then, the Sa'dan knew gambling only in the form of cock-fighting. Many of them, particularly the nobility, became addicted to these new games, with a markedly negative impact on the society as a whole.[51] The Bugis elicited ever higher taxes on gambling which the Sa'dan were in many cases unable to pay, often ending up as slaves as a result. Circa 1690 almost all of the inhabitants of the Sa'dan highlands came together as a unified force, defeating Arung Palakka's army. This event had vast historical importance for the Sa'dan, and to this day it is regarded as being of major significance.

The sources of the Bugis from Bone cite that in the years 1702 and 1705 they invaded the Sa'dan region again; at the same time, oral tradition among the Bugis of Luwu' has it that they participated in the 1702 invasion. Both groups concur that the Sa'dan recognized their sovereignty; the latter, however, vehemently denies any such version of this history, emphasizing instead that the armistice concluded in 1710 with the King of Bone. After the soldiers of Arung Palakka departed the Sa'dan Highlands, all contact between the Bugis and the Sa'dan ceased.

---

50   In the 15th century, Java was still entirely Hindu; Islam began to arrive on this territory only over the course of the 16th century.
51   *Tangdilintin* 1975, pp. 39–48.

2.2.5.3 The Coffee War and Its Consequences

After signing the peace treaty with Bone, the Sa'dan returned to their traditional way of life. Separate areas ruled by distinct customary laws (*adat*) continued to exist as independent and sovereign units.[52] It was only the latter half of the 19th century that brought major social changes to the area. The main point of contention and dispute between the Sa'dan and the Bugis, as well as the cause of feuds among separate groups in the Sa'dan Highlands itself, was the coffee trade. The crop was brought to this region by Bugis traders from the Alla district in the Duri region, who traded it with the Sa'dan in exchange for cotton fabrics. As coffee became more popular, two local kingdoms tried to win control of its production. The Sidenreng Kingdom has made a systematic effort to penetrate the coffee market in the Sad'an Highlands after 1885. The Luwu' Kingdom, however, was unwilling to relinquish their dominant position, resulting in struggles for monopoly between the two. Over time, Sidenreng also took control of trade, which until then had been conducted exclusively by Luwu'. In 1895 Sidenreng took total control of the coffee trade, and retained it even after the arrival of the Dutch.

The Coffee War in the late 19th century had a negative impact on both the social and political situation in the Sa'dan Highlands. After the Bugis introduced firearms to the local population, the Sa'dan, who had lived in peace for centuries, started to wage war amongst each other. Captured enemies were frequently sold into slavery, and there were numerous forced land seizures. The situation did not change until the arrival of the Dutch, when the Sa'dan were compelled to unify in order to be able to face up to them.

2.2.5.4 The Arrival of the Dutch to the Sa'dan Highlands

Although Indonesia had become a Dutch colony already at the beginning of the 17th century, and South Sulawesi was settled by the colonizers as early as in the middle of that same century, the first Dutch soldiers did not arrive in the Sa'dan Highlands until 1905.[53] In the years 1905–1906 the colonizers first subjugated the major lowland states one by one, including Bone, Sidenreng, Gowa and Luwu'. The second phase of the struggle focused on the conquest of the smaller lowland kingdoms, and finally their efforts culminated with the seizure of the mountain area of Sa'dan. In 1905 the Dutch succeeded in occupying almost all of South Sulawesi, a fact that exerted radical influence on the political climate

---

52 *Liku Ada'* 1986, pp. 39–41.
53 *Sandarupa* 2000, p. 18.

of the region. Wary of the Dutch army and foreseeing its advance, the top representatives of the Sa'dan agreed to unify in order to be able to stand up to the colonizers. Each leader had to build or restore their own fortifications on strategic elevated sites and furnish these with provisions and equipment, as well as upgrading their army. Despite these measures, they were all ultimately defeated, bringing the population of the Sa'dan Highlands in one fell swoop under colonial rule. The territory was divided into several administrative units controlled by supervisors appointed by the government. The activities of the first Dutch Protestant missionaries date to 1913; they built schools and fostered education among the Sa'dan. The growing level of education in the 1920s and 1930s contributed to the rise of ethnic awareness, and as a result the local "modern elites" started to refer to the Sa'dan Highlands as "Tana Toraja" – the land of the Toraja. Village schools commenced instruction of the standardized form of the Tae' language, i.e. Toraja, which first appeared in written form at this time. During these two decades, ethnic Toraja teachers replaced Malay-speaking pedagogues[54] who hailed from other parts of Indonesia and were appointed as part of the Dutch missions. After finishing school, many students stayed in the cities, and, free from the bonds of home and kin, started new families and began working away from their native villages. After they achieved an established status in the urban environment of the 1930s, awareness of ethnic identity among the Toraja radically intensified. The new Toraja identity involved an open anti-Bugis form of resistance and mutual solidarity. Dutch missionaries offered no hindrance to these tendencies by any means; on the contrary, they contributed to their propagation, accentuating the importance of defence against the eventuality of the Bugis threat. Christianity helped the Toraja to clearly define themselves as separate from the Muslim population inhabiting the lowlands.[55]

2.2.6 Language and Literature

In linguistic terms, Indonesia is an immensely diverse area and therefore it is important to briefly outline the linguistic situation in the Toraja region. The second part of the present section discusses literature, giving a more detailed account of Toraja language and traditions.

---

54 A standardized dialect of Malay was first declared the Indonesian language on October 28, 1928 in Batavia (today Jakarta) during the Youth Congress (*Sumpah Pemuda*). Their slogan was – One Motherland, One Nation, One Language. The event heralded the symbolic beginning of the struggle for the independence of Indonesia.

55 *Bigalke* 2005, pp. 178–179.

2.2.6.1 Linguistic Situation of the Toraja

To communicate among themselves, the Toraja use the Toraja language.[56] Linguists such as Cornelius Salombe define the language as Sa'dan Toraja, distinguishing three dialects within it: *Makale – Rantepao* in the east, *Saluputti – Bonggakaradeng* in the west, and *Sillinan – Gandang Batu* in the south.[57] The Toraja language has two forms: *bahasa pergaulan* (everyday language) which is used in routine communication, and *bahasa tominaa* (the language of the ceremonial priest *tominaa*) or *bahasa kesusasteraan* (literary language), designated for use on strictly defined occasions and spoken by select individuals.[58] *Bahasa tominaa* contains expressions and metaphors which many people, particularly the young, have trouble understanding, for it is a ritual language.[59] Alongside Toraja, Indonesian is also spoken as a language of communication in the Toraja region, and both languages belong to the Austronesian language group.[60] The distinct nature of both styles of Toraja is evident in the following example.[61]

Bahasa pergaulan (everyday language)	Bahasa tominaa (*tominaa* language)	English
baine	simbolong manik	girl
pare	tallu bulinna	rice in the field
tedong	sanglamba bulanna	water buffalo
siulu'ku	renden loloku	sibling

In urban areas, practically all inhabitants speak Indonesian. In isolated mountain villages, however, both older people who have never had the need or indeed the possibility to learn Indonesian, as well as children of pre-school age,

---

56 Some sources cite synonymous terms *Sa'dan* language, or *Tae'* language.
57 *Sandarupa* 2000, p. 3.
58 *Marampa'* (*Mengenal Toraja*), p. 39.
59 *Sandarupa* 1984, p. 4. This was confirmed during my field research. In Rantepao, I inquired about the language with several students of the STIKPAR (Sekolah Tinggi Kateketik dan Pastoral – Rantepao Catechetic and Pastoral Institute), and indeed, not a single one of them understood the language.
60 The Austronesian language group includes approximately 1 200 spoken languages, chiefly in the islands ranging from Madagascar to the Hawaiian and Easter Islands, including some territories in South-East Asia. It can be divided into four branches – Indonesian, Polynesian, Melanesian, and Micronesian.
61 *Marampa'* (*Mengenal Toraja*), p. 40.

have problems understanding it. Knowledge of the Indonesian language among first form pupils is close to zero, so that in reality teachers have to gradually replace Toraja with Indonesian, which is supposed to be the universal language of instruction from the first form, as is the case in Makale, Rantepao, and the rest of Indonesia.

After gaining independence in 1945, the politics of the Indonesian government regarding language was oriented towards the unification of the nation; instruction in local languages was therefore not encouraged. In the same year Indonesian – the *lingua franca* of the whole region – was declared the official language of Indonesia, yet it is actually the mother tongue of only a fraction of Indonesians. In the wake of political changes after 1965, the attitude of the government to the issue underwent a considerable change, and local languages are now taught as a separate subject in six-year grammar schools.

2.2.6.2 Literature on the Toraja Language and Toraja Traditions

The Toraja are an ethnic group without a written tradition, and therefore the knowledge of history, genealogy, traditions, ethics, and morals as well as religion was handed down in oral form from one generation to the next through means of prayers and oral poetry recited during a variety of rituals. These prayers in particular yield much information about the moral and spiritual as well as social aspects of Toraja culture. The seminal and most extensive of these is the *Passomba Tedong* – a prayer recited before the sacrifice of a buffalo during rituals of thanksgiving to the Gods.[62] It can only be recited by the *tominaa* (ceremonial priest), chosen by the consensus of the governing council. Everything related to the *Passomba Tedong* is regarded as sacred – its recitation, the content of the text, the maintenance of this custom as well as the ways of handing it down. The Toraja became introduced to writing primarily after the arrival of the Dutch at the beginning of the 20th century.[63] From the 1920s onwards, Toraja tales, genealogy, myths, songs, poems, rhymes and proverbs began to be published, and there also emerged various theses discussing Toraja language. The first authors to produce these were chiefly Dutch, later replaced by Toraja scholars.

---

62 These include for instance the rituals *merauk* and *ma'bua'* which are held next to a traditional Toraja house (*tongkonan* – see section 2.4.3) belonging to a kin group (*rapu*). In this prayer, they give thanks to their God and Creator *Puang Matua* as well as to the deities (*deata*) for favour shown to them. The *Passomba Tedong* includes a narrative of the creation of all living things as well as inanimate nature, together with various prescripts and injunctions (*Samban, Parinding et al.* 1988, p. 37).

63 In the 1890s most leaders could speak, write and read the Bugis language (*Bigalke* 2005, p. 34).

The first scholar to research local languages was the Dutch linguist Hendrik van der Veen (1888–1977). Beginning in 1916, he worked in Rantepao as well as other places in South and Central Sulawesi for nearly forty years. He was not sent to the region by the Gereformeerde Zendings Bond (Calvinist Mission Alliance, or GZB)[64] although he participated in its activities. He was nevertheless a representative of the Netherlands Bible Society (Nederlandsch Bijbelgenootschap). He studied Sa'dan Toraja and other south Toraja dialects, focusing on verbal folklore, which in his day was still essentially unrecorded.[65] In 1940 he published *Kamus Tae'-Belanda* [Toraja-Dutch Dictionary], and also translated the Bible into Sad'an Toraja for the Netherlands Bible Society, which was published four years after his return to the Netherlands in 1960. He was assisted by several Toraja, the scholars L. Pakan and J. Tammoe, among others.[66] In 1965 there appeared an anthology of ritual texts *Passomba Tedong* entitled *The Merok Feast of the Sa'dan Toradja* in the Toraja language, which he collected, edited and furnished with an English translation. One year later there followed a second volume entitled *The Sa'dan Toradja Chant for the Deceased*. The third volume, *Overleveringen en zangen der Zuid-Toradja's* [Traditions and Songs of the South Toraja] featuring an introduction and translation into Dutch came out only two years after the author's death, in 1979. It features six Toraja texts on the ancestry of the kings and songs accompanying various ceremonies and funeral rites. Van der Veen also co-authored several works together with A. A. van de Loosdrecht, the first Dutch Protestant pastor to be active in the Sa'dan region. Their collaborative efforts include: *Onder de Toradja's van Rante Pao* [Among the Toraja of Rante Pao] and *Voorloper spel- en leesboek in de Tae'-taal* [Primer and Reader of Tae' Language]. Thanks to numerous linguistic publications, the Sa'dan Toraja is one of the most thoroughly researched languages in South Sulawesi.

From the 1970s onward, the first works in linguistics by Toraja authors began to be published. One of the most prolific scholars is the linguist Cornelius Salombe, whose chief interest is Toraja morphology.[67] Another eminent researcher, J. S. Sande, focuses on folk poetry and oral literature, and, among

---

64   Gereformeerde Zendings Bond – a Protestant church society which spread the faith outside of the Netherlandish territory, founded in Utrecht, Netherlands, in 1902. The Dutch missionaries active in South and Central Sulawesi in the early years of the 20th century were mostly attached to the GZB.

65   As part of his missionary activities he also taught, and together with his wife, provided healthcare to the Toraja.

66   *Van den End* 1994, p. 17.

67   His works include for example *Proses Morfemis Kata Kerja Bahasa Toraja Saqdan* [Morphology of Verbs in Sa'dan Toraja] 1978, *Struktur Morfologi dan Sintaksis Bahasa Toraja Saqdan: Laporan Penelitian* [Morphological and Syntactic Structure of Sa'dan Toraja: Research Report] 1979, *Bahasa Toraja Saqdan: Proses Morfemis Kata Kerja* [Sa'dan Toraja: Morphology of Verbs] 1982, *Sistem Perulangan Bahasa Toraja Saqdan* [The System of Reduplication in Sa'dan Toraja] 1982.

other activities, collects folk tales, Toraja aphorisms and proverbs, as well as original Toraja poetry or chants accompanying the *badong* dances. His works analyse in particular the Toraja language and its structure, grammar, morphology and phonology.[68] Books have also been published on syntax, phonetics and phonology.[69] The last 20 years have produced fascinating linguistic studies (treatises as well as articles) oriented towards the comparative analysis of Toraja and other languages.[70] It is also worth mentioning publications discussing traditional sayings and fables of South Sulawesi. [71]

The present introductory and thus somewhat informational chapter offers an outline of the ethnic group residing in the Toraja region. I have discussed the origins of the population, the present understanding and etymology of the term *Toraja,* and the ethnic groups of the Toraja. I also furnish essential facts regarding the geography, climate and economy of the region which contribute to the basic picture of Toraja life, concluding with a word on the situation of Toraja language and culture in the 20th century. The information listed here is intended to facilitate basic insight into Toraja culture and to contribute to its understanding.

---

68 His works include for example *Himpunan Cerita Rakyat dalam Sastra Toraja* [Collected Folk Tales in Toraja Literature] 1981, *Seni Badong dalam Sastra Toraja* [The Art of the Badong in Toraja Literature] 1982, *Struktur Bahasa Toraja Sa'dan* [The Structure of Sa'dan Toraja] 1984, *Ungkapan dan Peribahasa Toraja* [Toraja Sayings and Proverbs] 1984, *Londe Puisi Asli Toraja* [Traditional Toraja Londe Poetry] 1986, *Passomba Tedong: Sastra Lisan Toraja* [Passomba Tedong: the Toraja Oral Folklore Tradition] 1986, *Morfologi Nomina Bahasa Toraja* [Morphology of Toraja Nouns] 1987, *Prosa Lirik Sastra Toraja* [Lyrical Prose in Toraja Folk Literature] 1989, *Sastra Toraja dan Terjemahannya* [Toraja Literature with Translation] 1990, *Verba Bahasa Toraja* [Toraja Verbs] 1994, *Tata Bahasa Toraja* [Toraja Grammar] 1997.

69 For example Badudu, J. S., *Fonetik dan Fonologi Bahasa Bare'e – Toradja di Sulawesi Tengah* [Phonetics and Phonology of Bare'e Toraja in Central Sulawesi] 1963.

70 For example Palinggi, O. O., *Analisis Kontrastif antara Fonem Bahasa Inggris dan Fonem Bahasa Toraja* [Contrastive Analysis of English and Toraja Phonemes] 1982.

71 For example Tangdilintin, L. T., *Ungkapan Tradisional Sebagai Sumber Informasi Kebudayaan Daerah Sulawesi Selatan* [Traditional Folk Sayings as a Source of Information on the Culture of South Sulawesi] 1984. Mustari, *Kumpulan Cerita Fabel Sulawesi Selatan* [Collected Fables of South Sulawesi] 1999.

Map of Indonesia

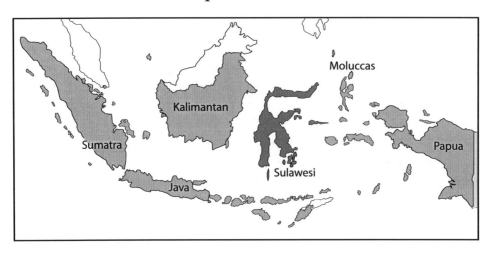

Map of Sulawesi

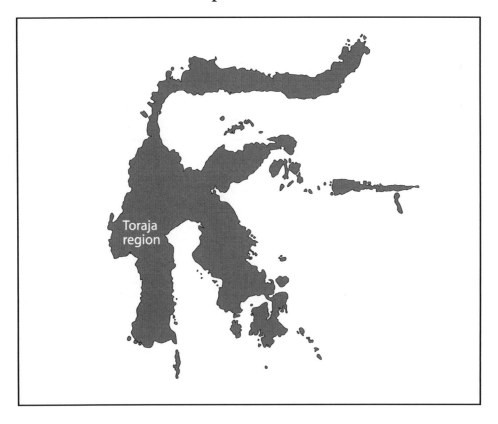

2.3 Autochthonous Religion *Aluk Todolo* and Adoption of Christianity

2.3.1 *Aluk Todolo* (*Alukta*)

The original religion of the Toraja is referred to as *Aluk Todolo* (the religion of the ancestors) or *Alukta*[72] and at present is adhered to by approximately 4% of the total population of the Toraja region.[73] In 1970 *Aluk Todolo* was recognized as a form of Hinduism and became one of the religions acknowledged by the state. It is based on a set of very strictly defined rules which have governed the everyday life of the Toraja since time immemorial. The concrete forms of this belief differ from region to region. Three elements, however, are regarded as the main spiritual pillars of the belief system: *Puang Matua* (the Old Lord),[74] *deata*[75] or deities, and *To Membali Puang* – the spirits of the ancestors. Deities – *deata* – were created by *Puang Matua* to rule in both heaven and earth and to oversee them. Depending on their sphere of influence, they are divided into the *Deata Tangngana Langi'* who rule heaven and the *Deata Kapadanganna*, who supervise activities on earth, and the *Deata Tangngana Padang*, which rule over the soil, sea, and rivers. Each of these three groups features a large multitude of further deities, each responsible for a specific place – a given mountain, river or forest. The spirits of the deceased ancestors *To Membali Puang* oversee the correct behaviour of their descendants and dispense blessings accordingly. The followers of *Aluk Todolo* therefore do not pray only to *Puang Matua* but also to the *deata* and to *To Membali Puang*. Depending on the nature of each rite, they sacrifice a prescribed number and species of animal (buffaloes, pigs and cocks/hens).[76]

In my study of the relevant literature I found various myths concerning the origin of the world, differing from one another in varying degrees depending on their region of origin. According to one version, the entire universe was created by God – *Puang Matua* – a view shared by my main informant *tominaa* Tato'

---

72 Several of my informants claimed, independently of one another, that this is a compound word of *aluk* (Tor.) – religion, and the suffix *ta* (Tor.), derived from the word *kita* (Tor.) meaning "we" or "ours". *Alukta* thus means "our religion". Adherents of Christianity prefer to use the term *Aluk Todolo,* expressing the fact that this is the belief of their ancestors and not their present religion. Nooy-Palm (1979, p. 107) nevertheless cites that the suffix *ta* may in fact be derived from the word *tau* (Tor.) – humankind. In this case, *Alukta* could be translated as the religion of humankind.

73 *Tana Toraja dalam Angka* [Tana Toraja in numbers] 2004, p. 46.

74 *Puang Matua* is conceived of either as the absolute Creator of the world, or at least of a large part of it.

75 Throughout the present work I will use the term deity to denote *deata* (Tor.), or *dewa* (Ind.), translating the word *Tuhan* (Ind.) as God.

76 *Tangdilintin* 1975, p. 55.

Dena', from the Mandetek region. According to a second theory mentioned for instance by Van der Veen, Nooy-Palm and Sandarupa, there first existed Heaven and Earth, who later created three gods; *Puang Matua* is considered to be the scion of the third generation of this progeny.

According to the first theory, the Sa'dan believed that their ancestors arose from divine beings, placed in heaven by *Puang Matua*.[77] The world as described by the cosmogonic myth was first a chaotic darkness without sun, moon, or stars, and heaven was connected to earth. When *Puang Matua* separated "the all-covering roof and the earthly region", he created his three children – *Pong Banggai Rante* (Vast Plain), *Pong Tulak Padang* (Supporter of the Earth), and *Gaun Tikembong* (Expanding Cloud). Under *Puang Matua's* supervision, his children conferred on their future duties and place of residence. The decisions had to be unanimous: this mythical consensus in the decision-making process was the celestial predecessor of all similar gatherings, *kombongan*.[78] All three children of *Puang Matua* agreed their mission was to care for humans and other living creatures. *Pong Banggai Rante* settled on the earth's surface, *Pong Tulak* in the core of the earth, and *Gaun Tikembong* chose the heavens. After a while he began to get lonely and thus applied to *Puang Matua* for help, who allowed him to extract a single rib from his body,[79] from which he created a man named *Usuk Sangbamban* (One Rib). The latter nonetheless also soon became lonely, roaming the heavens and looking for a wife. Suddenly he heard a comely female voice issuing from a rock and started to court the invisible maiden. She did not reject his advances but said that first a sacrifice *piong salampa*[80] had to be made to the highest god *Puang Matua*. When the rite was completed, there issued from the rock a ravishing maiden by the name of *Arang di Batu* (Radiance in the Rock).

Piong salampa was the first of the rites performed to worship *Puang Matua*, which collectively are universally known as *Aluk Rampe Matallo* (rites of the rising sun) or *Aluk Rambu Tuka'* (smoke ascending rituals). After this, *Puang Matua* ordered *Usuk Sangbamban* to create the first human. Using the *Sauan Sibarrung* bellows *Usuk Sangbamban* then cast a human form out of pure gold. The same forge was used to create the celestial ancestry of all living creatures and

---

77 *Samban, Parinding et al.* 1988, pp. 37–41. See the Genealogy of the Gods no. 1. I created this genealogy based on information from Samban, *Parinding et al.* (1988, pp. 37–41). I used the exact Toraja names and English translations of the Toraja names as provided in the text. The book does not specify the exact place of origin of this myth.

78 *Kombongan* (Tor.) – session, meeting. A system used throughout Indonesia, surviving to this day in the People's Consultative Assembly.

79 The motif is reminiscent of the Biblical narrative of Adam and Eve.

80 *Piong salampa* (Tor.) – offering in the form of bamboo filled with sticky rice. As a matter of fact, a traditional Toraja dish today is the *pa' piong* – meat and vegetable made in a bamboo shoot.

all of nature. The ancestor of the entire human race was *Datu Laukku'*[81] – who married *Bongga Langi'na*. For six generations, the descendants of this couple lived in heaven.

According to mythology, in the times when the world was in an ideal state, the celestial ladder *Eran Dilangi'* enabled a connection between heaven and earth.[82] One day *Puang Matua* decided to send to earth the 7,777 prescripts of the *Aluk Todolo*. He entrusted the task to a man by the name of *Puang Bura Langi'* and his wife *Kombong Bura*, who were accompanied on their journey by a slave named *Pong Pako Lando*. The journey ahead of them was full of extreme hardship and they decided to take with them only 777 prescripts. Once on earth, they settled in the Rura region, south of today's border of Tana Toraja. The couple conceived a son named *Pong Mula Tau*, who became the first human born on earth. He would later marry *Sanda Bilik* with whom he fathered two sons – *Londong di Langi'* and *Londong di Rura*.[83]

According to one version, *Londong di Rura* had four children, two sons and two daughters. Since the parents could not find partners for them, they sent a pair of slaves to ask the god *Puang Matua* whether marriage between blood relatives was allowed. The journey to heaven was too long and gruelling, however, so the slaves never reached God. Returning to their master they nonetheless led him to believe that such a marriage was possible.[84] The marriage incensed *Puang Matua* and the raging god then flooded the entire site of the wedding ceremony.[85] Following this, the brother of *Londong di Rura*, that is, *Londong di Langi'*, was summoned to heaven, where *Puang Matua* gave him four nuts of the areca palm tree which he was told to plant. The first of those nuts was in one piece, the second was split into halves, the third was split into quarters, and the last was split into eighths. If the first nut had grown into a plant, it would have meant that siblings can intermarry. Cousins were to be allowed to marry in case the second nut took root as well. If the third nut took, this would grant permission for their children to marry one another, and the fourth nut flourishing would enable marriage between descendants whose grandparents were cousins. After *Londong di Langi'* returned to earth, the ladder was broken so that heaven was no longer accessible to humans. One month after planting all four nuts, *Londong di Langi'* found that the first of them went to rot; the

---

81   In this case, the first human was of female gender; however, tradition in other parts of the Toraja region has it that *Datu Laukku'* was a man.

82   Thus only the descent to earth separated celestial and earthly human beings.

83   *Sandarupa* 2000, p. 15.

84   Toraja mythology features this notorious motif: a lie as the original sin.

85   Flooding as the expression of the wrath of God in response to the sinful behaviour of humans appears in many cultures. The oldest written record of this sort of disaster appears in the Epic of Gilgamesh.

remaining three nonetheless grew. This meant that marriage between siblings was inadmissible, while marriage between cousins as well as progeny whose parents or grandparents were cousins, was allowed.[86]

Another version cites that *Londong di Rura* became a successful farmer and father of eight children, four sons and four daughters. Desirous that his property remained in the family, he married his sons to his daughters. This presumptuous act defied the law and made *Puang Matua* indignant. As a punishment, he flooded the whole of the Rura region, where the weddings took place. The only one spared was *Londong di Langi'* who had discouraged his brother from going through with the marriage. *Puang Matua* bid him to find the hermit named *Suloara'* (Spiritual Torch) who would be able to show the correct path to those who had survived. According to mythology, from that time *Suolara'* is regarded as the bearer of light and deliverer of the Toraja, their saviour and teacher of the morals dictated by the Divine.[87]

According to another version of the myth,[88] which, as in Nooy-Palm, is passed down in the Kesu' region and recorded in the *Passomba Tedong*,[89] there initially existed only Heaven and Earth. Their sacred union gave rise to the entire world. They had three children: *Pong Tulakpadang* (Supporter of the Earth) – god of the Underworld, *Pong Banggairante* (Vast Plain) – the god of Earth, and *Gauntikembong* (Self Expanding Cloud) – god of the Air. *Gauntikembong* removed his rib and from it made *Usuk Sangbamban*, who married *Simbolong Manik*, also named *Lokkon Lo-Erara'*. They had a son named *Puang Matua* who was thus the scion of the third generation of the original divine couple of Heaven and Earth. According to this version of the myth, *Puang Matua* is not the creator of the entire world, but is still regarded as an important deity. To him is attributed the creation of the first man, whose life he oversaw and whom he made mortal. When humans departed from good morals, committing incest and theft in violation of his commandments, *Puang Matua* severed the heavens from earth. The verses of the *Passomba Tedong* indicate that *Puang Matua* always had a privileged status among all the other gods, and after the arrival of Christianity he gained even greater prominence.[90]

He resides in the heart of the firmament;
he is the god of the dazzling sun;

---

86   *Sandarupa* 2000, pp. 15–16.
87   *Samban, Parinding et al.* 1988, p. 40.
88   See the Genealogy of the Gods no. 2. This genealogy of the gods of Kesu' is taken from *Nooy-Palm* (1979, p. 132). I used the English translations of the Toraja names as provided in the text.
89   The ritual texts *Passomba Tedong* were published by Hendrik van der Veen in 1965 under the title *The Merok Feast of the Sa'dan Toradja* – see section 2.2.6.
90   *Nooy-Palm* 1979, pp. 118 and 134–135.

he is the god whom the honoured ancestors (the *nene'* and the *to dolo*)
   solicit to partake when the sacrifice stands ready;

he has laid out the irrigated ricefields, indicated where the offering places
   for the rice should be;

he created the three-eared rice and he created mankind, the forefather of
   the water buffalo, etc.;

he formed the sun; he cut out the moon as a circle, he made the clouds,
   and caused the roar of thunder;

he is associated with the zenith.[91]

Puang Matua married the goddess *Arrang diBatu* (The Radiance in the Stone). His wife sent him on a quest of gold, of which he would – using the *Sauan Sibarrung* bellows – make the first human, *Datu Laukku'* (in this myth from the Kesu' region, the first human is also a woman) and seven other living creatures.[92] These were *Allo Tiranda* – the ancestor of the poisonous *ipo'* tree (Antiaris toxicaria Lesch), *Laungku* – the ancestor of cotton, *Pong Pirik-Pirik* – the ancestor of rain, *Menturiri*[93] – the ancestor of fowl, *Manturini* – the forefather of the buffalo, *Riako'* – the ancestor of iron, *Takkebuku* [94] – the ancestor of rice. The ash that remained from the creation of these eight siblings was scattered and various trees grew from it.[95] After this, *Puang Matua* created six descendants in the same manner. One of these was *Kambunolangi'* (Sunshade of the Firmament) – the first *tominaa* (ceremonial priest), who was attributed the status of a demigod. The progeny of his brother[96] – *Datu Bakka'* and *Pong Malaleong* had an entirely different social status, as they became the first slaves. The younger siblings included *Pande Patangnga'* (The One Who is Capable of Skilful Planning), *Pande Pandita* or *Pande Paita* (The Skilful Seer), *Pande Manarang* (Master Carpenter), and *Pande Paliuk* (Extra-Ordinarily Skilled). The *Passomba Tedong* goes on to describe how *Puang Matua* created the *sawah* (irrigated fields) and introduced a variety of rituals (the rice ritual, the *maro*

---

91 *Nooy-Palm* 1979, p. 119.
92 See the Genealogy of the Gods no. 3. I compiled the genealogy based on information in *Nooy-Palm* (1979, pp. 136–137) and *Sandarupa* (1984, pp. 29–30). I used the English translations of the Toraja names as provided in the texts.
93 *Sandarupa* (1984, p. 29) cites *Menturini*.
94 *Tangdilintin* (1975, p. 53) cites *Irako* instead of *Riako*. Instead of the predecessor of boiled rice – *Takkebuku* – he cites the predecessor of uncooked rice, *Lamemme*. Indonesian uses different terms for rice as a crop (*padi*), grains of uncooked rice (*beras*) and cooked rice (*nasi*).
95 *Nooy-Palm* 1979, p. 136.
96 *Nooy-Palm* (1979, p. 137) does not mention the name of the brother of *Kambunolangi'*, whose children were called *Datu Bakka'* and *Pong Malaleong*. She nevertheless goes on to mention four other siblings of *Kambunolangi'*. Sandarupa (1984, p. 30) offers the same account, citing as the sixth person *Pande Nunu*. I thus assume that *Pande Nunu* was the father of *Datu Bakka'* and *Pong Malaleong*.

ritual to heal the infirm, the *bua'* ceremony celebrating a good harvest and the well-being of the community, and the *merok* ritual performed by an individual or an entire kin group – *rapu* – as an expression of thanks for their prosperity), and stipulated specifically what animals are to be sacrificed during each rite. The conclusion of this prayer cites *Puang Bura Langi'* and *Kembong Bura* descending on earth together with the slave *Pong Paku Lando,* bringing with them the 777 rules of *Aluk Todolo*.[97]

Aluk Todolo existed in two autochthonous versions, as *Aluk Sanda Pitunna* (Complete Seven Religious Rules), which emerged approximately in the 10th century, and *Aluk Sanda Saratu'* (Complete Hundred Religious Rules) dating from the 13th century. *Aluk Sanda Pitunna* was also referred to as *Aluk Patang Pitu* – the commandments of the four sevens (7,777) or *Aluk Pitung Sa'bu Pitu Ratu' Pitung Pulo Pitu* – Seven Thousand Seven Hundred and Seventy-Seven Religious Rules (7,777), or even *Aluk Pitung Pitu* – the Religious Rules of the Seven Sevens (7,777,777).[98] It is evident, that the actual number of religious precepts (*aluk*) was irrelevant, with the number seven being purely symbolic, expressing their abundance and simultaneously alluding to the number of the *aluk* (commandments) originally sent to earth by *Puang Matua*. The *Aluk Sanda Pitunna* (Complete Seven Religious Rules) was spread above all thanks to *Tangdilino'*, scion of the sixth generation of *Londong di Langi'* and his wife *Tumba'*. *Tangdilino'* is regarded as one of the most important ancestors in many *rapu* (kin groups). He famously disagreed with the form of government in the Rura region, ruled by a nobleman who used the title *Puang* (God). He found this social structure to be too monarchical and therefore moved north to the Mengkendek region,[99] where he established a more democratic system, introducing the title *Ma'dika*[100] (Freeman) instead of the title *Puang* (God).[101]

Aluk Sanda Saratu' (Complete Hundred Religious Rules) was brought by the *tomanurun* (people descended from heaven),[102] led by *Puang Tamboro Langi'* approximately in the 13th century. *Aluk Sanda Saratu'* drew on *Aluk Sanda Pitunna*

---

97 *Nooy-Palm* 1979, pp. 136–138.
98 *Liku Ada'* 1986, p. 26.
99 *Tangdilino'* was instrumental in the erection of the illustrious traditional house – *tongkonan* – Banua Puan in the village of Marinding in the Mengkendek region (*Nooy-Palm* 1979, pp. 25 and 76).
100 *Ma'dika* corresponds to the Indonesian term *merdeka* – free.
101 *Tangdilintin* 1975, p. 10.
102 The *tomanurun* arrived in the territory of present-day Tana Toraja and Toraja Utara at some point around the 13th century. The local population was astonished by the scope of their knowledge and skills, concluding that the new arrivals must be demigods coming from Heaven. The most famous *tomanurun* were *Manurun di Langi' di Kesu'*, *Tamboro Langi' di Kandora* and *Mambio Langi' di Kaero* (*Tangdilintin* 1975, p. 19). To this day, the origin of these "celestial beings" (*tomanurun*) remains unclear but it is assumed they most likely came from eastern Java, from the Singhasari Kingdom under the rule of King Kertanagara.

(based on the cementing of the bond between man and both *deata* and the god *Puang Matua*). However, there was a new emphasis on the secular social system.[103] *Aluk Sanda Saratu'* caught on particularly in the south, in the localities of Makale, Sangalla' and Mengkendek.

The Toraja believed that the *aluk*, commandments, which dictated norms of behaviour, were sent to them directly from heaven. Along with the *aluk*, there nonetheless also came to earth the *pemali* – a system of injunctions, the violation of which was met by a strictly defined punishment. Some of these are very reminiscent of the Christian Decalogue: *Pemali ma'pangan buni* – Thou shall not commit adultery! *Pemali Boko* – Thou shall not steal! Others are, on the contrary, reflections of the most characteristic features of Toraja culture, defined by social stratification and the great importance of death rites: *Pemali unteka' palanduan* – Members of different social classes must not marry. *Pemali urrusak pote di bolong* – Nothing can disrupt the funeral ceremony, and the burial of the deceased must not be disrupted. There were countless *pemali* (injunctions) and in the past it was regarded as essential that all members of Toraja society observed them to the letter; there was even a *to ma'pemali* – a specific person responsible for overseeing that they were observed.

2.3.2 Social and Ceremonial Roles in *Aluk Todolo* Rituals

Aluk Todolo distinguished several types of ceremonial priests, each of whom performed different rituals and operations.[104] Nooy-Palm cites that they were divided into six basic categories: *tominaa* and *tomenani*, whom I shall discuss later, *to indo' padang*, *to mebalun*, *to burake tattiku'* and *to ma'dampi*. The *to indo' padang* would perform rituals related to the cultivated soil (rice fields). *To mebalun* was responsible for the wrapping of the bodies of the deceased, and was regarded as a pariah. *To burake tattiku'* were exclusively women, and *to burake tambolang* was a man cross-dressed as a woman; both performed their ceremonial role during the *bua'* rite, which celebrated a good harvest and the well-being of the community. The role of *to ma'dampi* could be performed by either a man or a woman endowed with healing powers – they would participate in the purifying rituals *maro* and *ma'bugi*.[105]

The present work deals only with the *tominaa* and *tomenani*, I shall therefore discuss them in some detail. Traditionally, the most important ceremonial priest

---

103 *Liku Ada'* 1986, p. 30.
104 At present there are only a handful of these ceremonial priests.
105 *Nooy-Palm* 1979, p. 274.

was the *tominaa* (lit. a moral man; a wise man) who participated in a large part of all rituals – distinguished by an exceptional memory (able to recite lengthy prayers by heart), he was well versed in both mythology and common law. Nooy-Palm[106] in fact mentions that in the Kesu' region, the recital of the *Passomba Tedong* prayer preceding the sacrifice of buffaloes during the *merok* ritual (an individual or a whole kin group – *rapu* – express their thanks to God for their prosperity) lasted no less than twelve hours. In the times when the Toraja were not literate, it was in fact due to the lore of the *tominaa* that Toraja culture was able to be passed down orally from one generation to the next. The *tominaa* Tato' Dena' cited that a member of any social class could become a ceremonial priest,[107] and that the role was not hereditary, yet it often passed from father to son, being the exclusive province of men. An aspirant had to be intelligent, be able to memorize all that was necessary, as well as be endowed with the special power of his prayers being heard. Tato' Dena' cited as example of this a situation where by an application to God, *tominaa* manages to heal an ailing person. The candidate further must have been able to perform a whole number of ceremonies, and only after mastering these would he win the right to be titled as *tominaa*.

Unlike the *tominaa,* the office of the *tomenani* ceremonial priest was hereditary, and could be held by a woman. The *tomenani*, who could only be succeeded by a blood relation, possessed various heirlooms; typical items were brass horns which he or she wore while performing rituals. In earlier times when marriage between social classes was banned, the *tomenani* hailed from the highest rank, *tana' bulaan*. At present, however, it is unlikely that there is anyone whose ancestors originate from a single social class. This is naturally also true for the *tomenani*. When questioning my informant as to further differences between the *tominaa* and *tomenani*, he merely cited that not every *tominaa* is a *tomenani*, but every *tomenani* is by default also a *tominaa*. In the Tallulembangna region a *tomenani* is addressed with the title *Ne' Sando*. At the moment, Tato' Dena' is the sole *Ne' Sando* in the whole region. He claims that both *tominaa* and *tomenani* help the adherents of *Aluk Todolo* to materialize their wishes and supplications derived from this religion.

In earlier times, another important person in the performance of rituals who nonetheless did not play the role of a ceremonial priest was the local ruler, *to parengnge'* (lit. the man carrying a burden). His office was hereditary much like the office of *tomenani*. According to my informant Tato' Dena', unlike the *tominaa*, who provided the spiritual connection with God through prayer and

---

106 *Nooy-Palm* 1986, p. 275.
107 In earlier times, Toraja society was very strictly stratified – see section 2.4.1.

offerings, the role of the *to parengnge'* was to provide for the material side of the ritual. Thus in the *bua'* rites celebrating a successful harvest, he had to provide items such as betel, rice, a rooster or a pig, or even a buffalo. As a token of respect and gratitude, he would receive large portions of meat from the sacrificed animals during the funeral rites. Tato' Dena' took objection to the present situation, where a considerable part of the *to parengne'* – local rulers – had converted, which to a large degree changed their perception of their duties. He disapprovingly observed that some of the present *to'parengnge* merely exploit their status (receiving large portions of meat from the animals sacrificed during funeral rites, or governing village affairs) while neglecting their duties as set forth by the *Aluk Todolo*, as they are now Christian.

2.3.3 The *Pesung* (Offerings)

During the *Aluk Todolo* rituals, the animals (mostly roosters, hens, pigs and buffaloes) are sacrificed to the deities and the ancestors. Each animal thus sacrificed must be prepared as an offering – *pesung* (see Figs. 8, 9). Christians have abandoned the custom entirely, for the *pesung* is indisputably a part of the *Aluk Todolo* religion, and therefore they cannot continue to practice this custom.

The number and combination of sacrifices as well as the cardinal direction (dictated by the position of the traditional house) to which the *pesung* is placed, all depend on the type of ritual. Still, certain attributes of the *pesung* always remain identical – the underside is always formed by half of a banana leaf, upon which are placed two layers (the lower larger than the upper) of rectangular slices of banana leaf (as a rule 4–8 pieces); piled on top of them are the flesh of different body parts of the sacrificed animal, bones as well as boiled blood, rice, betel leaf, areca nut and lime.[108] After this, the priest performing the ritual (most often a *tominaa*) sprinkles the *pesung* with palm wine, carrying separate parts to strictly prescribed places in the vicinity. Presently the *tominaa* drinks palm wine from bamboo, the gesture denoting that the preparation of the first *pesung* is at an end and the preparation of a second, or even a third *pesung* may commence. The deities to whom the *pesung* is addressed take from it "all that is necessary", after which it can be eaten by either humans or animals. The *tominaa* Tato' Dena' claimed that if consumed by pregnant women, such a repast may have magical effects.

---

108 Slaked powder lime.

Interview no. 1

M. B.:[109] So when the ritual is over, can people eat the betel leaf and areca nut?

T. D.:[110] They can, they can. The *pesung* is usually eaten by pregnant women, when they want their child to be pretty.

M. B.: Offerings like betel leaf, areca nut or rice and chicken?

T. D.: Pregnant women will eat the rice and chicken from the *pesung*. Once I said to a young woman in Enrekang that I would perform a ritual like this one.[111] The woman happened to be black, she was the wife of my nephew. Her sister was pregnant, both she and her husband were from Flores, so they were both completely black.[112] I called to her, "Come, I will give you the *pesung*, so that your child is white." She hesitated, saying, "Is that possible?" – "Why not?", I said. When her child was born, she cried in the hospital that her child was as white as the western race, like you are. She said, "I gave birth to a Dutch baby girl[113] thanks to Nene' Tato'." [*Laughs.*] The child is spirited, she never wants to lose. So who knows, she is probably in school now, but she always comes looking for me. When she came here first, she would say, "I want to kiss Nene' Sando, where is he?" She embraced me and said, "Thanks to you I am beautiful." [*He laughs.*]

The *pesung,* which were formerly an integral part of all rituals, are now found to a very limited extent, since they are practiced only by the followers of *Aluk Todolo*. Thus at present there are only very few priests able to prepare the *pesung* in keeping with all the strict ancestral rules.

2.3.4 The Adoption of Christianity

2.3.4.1 The Arrival of Christianity and the Founding of the First Protestant Schools[114]

Although the first Christian missionaries appeared in Indonesia as early as the 16th century, shortly after the arrival of Portuguese and Dutch traders, they

---

109 Michaela Budiman.

110 Tato' Dena'.

111 The *tominaa* had just finished one of the many rituals connected with the building of a house, in the course of which he sacrificed a rooster.

112 Most Indonesians yearn for as pale a complexion as possible.

113 Tato' Dena' used the term *Belanda* (Ind.) – Dutchman, which is to this day a synonym for a white man in general. In colonial times, the Dutch were practically the only white people Indonesians were in contact with.

114 The historical data cited in this subsection are gleaned from the Indonesian publication of *Van Schie* (2000, pp. 19–47).

did not reach what is today Tana Toraja and Toraja Utara until as late as 1913. They followed Dutch soldiers who had gained political control of the territory (1905–1907). At the end of 1913, the colonial administration granted the Gereformeerde Zendings Bond (GBZ) permission to work in the *onderafdeeling*[115] of Rantepao and Palopo, and six months later also in the *onderafdeeling* of Makale. The first proselytizer of Christianity in Rantepao and Palopo was A. A. van de Loosdrecht. His activity in the area, however, was not long-lived, as on July 26, 1917 he was murdered by Ne' Matandung – the head of the Balusu district. What is surprising, however, is the fact that the murder was motivated by political rather than religious reasons. As Ne' Matandung later confessed, his intended target was not Van de Loosdrecht but instead the state official who served as the head of the *onderafdeeling*. It can thus be said that even though the adoption of Christianity did not occur without problems, it was far more difficult for the Toraja to come to terms with foreign hegemony, which they had not known until that point.

Christianity established itself gradually and non-violently. At first the Dutch founded schools, which had not existed in the Toraja region previously. As required by A. A. van de Loosdrecht, the Toraja themselves had to physically contribute to the construction of these schools. In 1920 the colonial administration introduced school fees, which were largely not accepted, and thus in 1931 they issued a new measure requiring payment of these school fees. However, this brought little significant change, as many people at that time had no ready money. This fact is affirmed in the following interview by four older Toraja women who mostly attended school in the 1930s.

Interview no. 2

M. B.: Did you have to pay school fees back then (*at the time you attended school*)?

P. T. R. A.:[116] Yes, we did. Back then I had a grandfather in Makale, and when the fees were due, I visited him in an office in Makale, bringing him a letter in which we asked him to give me money to pay for my school. The fee was twenty five cents.

M. B.: Twenty five cents per month?

P. T. R. A.: Yes, per month.

M. B.: How much was a kilogram of rice in those days? [*I asked about the price of rice on purpose, since the Toraja, as is the case with virtually all Indonesians, eat rice as a rule three times a day. I thus assumed that the women might remember its price.*]

---

115 This administrative unit roughly corresponds to a county.
116 Puang Toding Rante Allo.

P. T. R. A.: It was still cheap back then. When my parents were still alive, things were still cheap; you didn't have so many people back then. If you had five people to a household that was a lot back then. [*The total population in those days was naturally smaller than today, but the traditional family actually is receding now. In those times, the average family had approximately ten children, for the Toraja believed that a great number of children was a sign of divine favour. One's children maintained the continuity of the family as well as providing a welcome workforce, particularly in the fields.*]

M. B.: So how much was a kilogram of rice?

P. T. R. A.: It was cheap.

M. B.: I ask because I want to get an idea how much that was compared with the school fees.

P. T. R. A.: We actually never bought rice; we grew it ourselves.

[*A conclusion reached after a short discussion in Toraja.*]

M. B.: And when you wanted to buy a buffalo?

P. T. R. A.: A buffalo was a hundred and fifty cents. We did not need to buy rice, so we didn't know what it actually cost. We had our own rice.

The interview indicates that the grandfather who lived in a city was probably the only person in the family to have ready money. His relatives in the village had no cash. I did not manage to verify the information on the price of school fees and that of a buffalo; however, what is important for the present work is the fact that during this period, common people indeed did not have money and thus could not pay school fees, as is supported by the responses of the older Toraja women. Their assertion corresponds with another interview[117] where I tried to find out at which point a man of nearly ninety years of age converted to Christianity. As he could not recall the date, I tried to prompt his memory by means of some clue, asking him whether he was already in school at that point. Evidently taken aback, he laughed saying that at the time, (that is, in the early 1920s) only wealthy people went to school, as ordinary farmers did not have money to pay the fees.[118] The situation gradually changed and the numbers of pupils grew, although parents often sent children to school only with great reluctance – as it cost them both money and the labour the child would have provided for their fields. They also rightly feared that the influence of Christian education would eventually cause their offspring to convert.

---

117 The interview was conducted in Toraja through an interpreter. The respondent spoke no Indonesian and my grasp of Toraja is that of a beginner.
118 The Pentecostal Pastor Yunus Padang mentions that parents sometimes had to sell a buffalo in order to be able to pay for school fees.

2.3.4.2 Disputes Between Protestant and Catholic Churches

In 1930 the Gereformeerde Zendings Bond (GZB) already ran as many as 73 three-year grammar schools, one follow-up school in Makale where instruction was conducted in Malay, and one five-year Dutch school. In the same year, they also opened a course in preaching featuring a lecture entitled "False Religions, i.e., Animism, Islam and the Catholic Doctrine."[119] One of the comments made on Catholicism in connection with this was that "The Catholics get around everywhere and it is certain that eventually we shall have to compete with them even in these parts."[120] The local Dutch Protestants were worried that Catholics would ultimately broach their territory. The first Catholic priest to enter the present-day Tana Toraja and Toraja Utara was the Jesuit Father H. Leemker SJ in 1910.[121] During his several-day visit he also served the first Catholic mass[122] before returning to Makassar. In 1925 the Catholics applied for permission to be able to set up missions in several locations in South and Central Sulawesi. They repeated their petition several more times without success; they were finally granted permission only in 1927, for the Banggai territory.[123] The consent to allow Catholic missions on this territory was probably intended to eliminate their efforts to penetrate into the Sa'dan region. In the late 1920s and early 1930s Catholic priests made several visits to the locality, each time baptising several believers (at the same period, the Sa'dan were also baptised in Makassar). At the beginning of the 1930s, ideological squabbles broke out between Protestants who feared the loss of their ecclesiastic monopoly and Catholics who did everything in their power to penetrate the Sa'dan highlands. The Protestants claimed that the Catholics used gifts to bribe the Sa'dan to convert to Catholicism. Catholics naturally protested that they never employed such practices, saying that they merely made occasional small donations of money to the poor. In 1932 the deputy governor inquired of the Protestants whether he should grant the Catholics permission to set up missionary activities. The Protestants vehemently defended their position, arguing that the Catholics would disrupt their hitherto successful activity. They would disorient the recently converted Sa'dan, which could lead to political

---

119 "Agama palsu, yakni Animisme, Islam dan ajaran Gereja Roma" (*Van Schie* 2000, p. 25).
120 "Roma memaksa masuk ke mana-mana dan pasti lama-lama di sini pun kita akan harus bersaing dengan dia" (*Van Schie* 2000, p. 25).
121 Since at that time the roads had not yet been built, the priest first sailed from Makassar to Palopo, continuing on foot across the mountains all the way to Rantepao.
122 *Van Schie* (2000, p. 21) cites that efforts to find out in which house the mass was celebrated failed. The book likewise does not mention for whom it was served. I believe that it was perhaps for Catholics who originated in other parts of Indonesia, where Catholicism had arrived earlier.
123 The island is part of Central Sulawesi.

instability in the region. On the strength of this argument as well as other critical voices, the Catholic petition was once again rejected. In spite of this, in the years 1937–1938, the Catholics began to slowly prepare themselves for their mission, buying lands and a house for the priest as well as launching the construction of their first school.[124] They finally succeeded in obtaining permission for residency and missionary activities in 1939. The first priest to settle in Makale on a permanent basis was Chris Eykemans.

The Catholics proceeded much as the Protestants had – first of all focusing on building schools. Their first three-year grammar school was built in the village of Kampo on the request of local inhabitants, but due to a vocal opposition of the Protestants, who appealed the matter as far as Makassar, the school soon closed down. Trouble also plagued the construction of other educational facilities. It is hardly surprising that the Protestants begrudged the fact that Catholics charged no school fees. The Protestants had put in tremendous effort in order to persuade the Toraja of the importance of education; once they had actually succeeded in doing so and parents started sending their children to school, there suddenly appeared a rival educational system, one offering tuition free of charge. Some parents transferred their children to a Catholic school solely for economic reasons. In response to the situation, the Protestants erected three grammar schools with free tuition of their own in sites designated for new Catholic educational institutions. Despite considerable financial difficulties they actually set up seven new schools in 1939. The situation finally came to the point where an inspection committee, which attempted to settle the strife between both parties, ordered that no new school could be built within a radius of five kilometres from an existing school. It further banned transfers of pupils to another school. Despite these economic problems, the Catholics succeeded in opening subsequent schools in Rantepao and Makale, which played a huge role in the spread of Catholicism.[125]

---

124 Surprisingly, however, the first Catholic teacher was the Toraja Petrus Pemba in 1938, albeit on an unofficial basis. A layman hailing from Tampo Makale, after graduating from grammar school he enrolled on the next level in Makale. His parents were in the habit of dispensing frequent corporal punishment and thus one day he did not return home, instead taking up with the director of the Protestant school. Later he moved to Palopo and eventually to Minahasa, where he continued his studies. Although his adoptive father was a Protestant, Petrus himself became a Catholic. In 1938 he returned to his native village Tampo Makale, where he started teaching children Christianity through songs and games in an area underneath his house (traditional Toraja houses are built on pylons, the space between them was formerly used for keeping cattle). In spite of being accused of running an illegal school several times, each time he was able to successfully defend himself against the charge.
125 At that point the church was not yet sponsored by its members. Financial subsidies from the Vatican were minimal, ceasing entirely after the outbreak of the Second World War.

2.3.4.3 The Process of Conversion to Christianity

Among other things, it transpired from the interviews that I have done that in the past the vast majority of converts were children attending Christian schools. Their parents would most often learn about Christianity second-hand from their progeny and their teachers. In the rural areas, teachers were fairly close to the pupils and their parents. Teachers would sometimes visit with the pupils' families, particularly if the children did not attend school. On such informal occasions, the teachers would disseminate the new religion, much like priests and catechists. Later, the notions of Christianity would naturally be handed down from one generation to the next. With rare exceptions, most adults had a negative attitude to Christianity – unlike their children.[126] The people I approached mostly claimed that their parents were angry and forbade them to convert. The children, however, were enthralled by the new religion. Sometimes they would go as far as becoming baptised without their parents knowing, for some priests did not insist on parental consent (although in most cases they did). One of the women I interviewed cited that her longing for Christianity was so strong that in defiance of her parents' explicit disapproval, she secretly attended religious classes.

The memories of my informants offer diverse reflections of the Toraja's initial contact with Christianity. Many were exceedingly struck by Biblical narratives; the Dutch missionaries were probably accomplished storytellers. The Pentecostal pastor Yunus Padang gives the following account of the situation at the time: "Every morning we sang religious songs and once a week they told us stories from the Bible, of the Creation, of Joseph, I used to love that. [*His intonation betrayed powerful emotion.*] To this day, those stories are alive in my memory. The school was in fact a place where faith was disseminated." He further cited that children liked to visit the pastors as they would get bread, cheese and chocolate from them – delicacies unknown to the Toraja in those days. My informant Martha Pudi said: "We were enthralled by religion [*What she meant was the religion that was new to the Toraja – Christianity.*] We used to learn about religion in school all the time – of Our Lord Jesus Christ, his nativity, and so on." The people I interviewed would also often mention that they were intrigued by the decoration of churches (particularly Catholic ones) and their sacral atmosphere, the scent of incense as well as the priests' vestments. For instance, it was for this reason that Yasinta Rumengan Ronting, at that time aged eleven, converted from Protestantism to Catholicism at the incitement of her Catholic cousin. Even decades later, she was still visibly proud that she had followed the "voice

---

126 Only a fraction of my informants cited that their parents consented to their conversion.

of her heart" – as she put it – choosing Catholicism though still a child. Prior to this momentous event, she had attended a Protestant grammar school and was shortly to be baptised. However, when her teacher wanted to prepare her for baptism, she dissembled that she had not been given permission by her parents, an excuse which the tolerant pedagogue accepted. With this deception, Ms. Ronting went through the rest of her six-year attendance, after which she told her parents the truth and they enrolled her in a Catholic secondary school. She was baptised in her second year, at the age of fourteen. In a recapitulation of our interview, I reached the conclusion that the main reason Ms. Ronting had converted to Christianity at that time was her visual enchantment with clerical vestments. My informant nonetheless protested that she was much struck by the devotional atmosphere of the church and the liturgical proceedings in which the mass was performed, despite never having mentioned these two factors before. I believe that the sacrament of baptism was also a great enticement for children. Although Ms. Ronting had been baptised nearly half a century before, her account of the affair was rich in detail[127] and full of enthusiasm even after all those years. Gisberta Balla Tandiau' cited another reason for conversion: "Many children around us converted, so we wanted to do so too. In spite of our parents forbidding it, we still converted."

Although the attitude to *Alukta* differed with various churches, Christian missionaries generally strove to spread the view that the original religion had become archaic and should be abandoned as such. Thus at present, most people see the *Alukta* as a relic of the past, as the religion of the ancestors, something which has become obsolete and replaced by the "superior and more advanced" religion of Christianity. Most of my respondents were laconic on the subject, quickly moving to another topic, like Martha Pudi in the following extract.

Interview no. 3

M. B.: Back home in your village everyone still followed *Alukta*, practising *Alukta* rituals, but you were taught differently at school. How did you feel about that?

M. P.:[128] I had parted with customary law and have observed Christianity ever since, that was what interested me. [*Having done with it in one sentence, she then*

---

127 She also mentioned that younger and older children would sit together during special classes preparing them for baptism. She remembered the names of both priests who prepared them for the occasion. She knew which one of them baptised the older and the younger children. She recounted how together with her cousin they chose their Christian names and how they giggled during baptism. She remembered her classmate, a boy, who chose the name Maria, which the teacher than changed to Marianos.

128 Martha Pudi.

talked about her parents.] But in spite of being a man of the customary law [*In spite of adhering to the indigenous religion*], my father was not angry at all. My mother, on the other hand, was indignant. But he said: "We cannot be angry with the child. We shall not stand in the way of what she loves." That was a great thing he did.

The terms used by the Christians today to denote the followers of *Alukta* speak volumes. Alongside the term *orang Alukta*, which could be loosely translated as an adherent of *Alukta*, I frequently also noted the designation *orang yang belum masuk Kristen* – a person who had not yet converted to Christianity, *orang yang belum masuk agama* – a person who had not yet embraced religion, *orang apa namanya?* – "those, what do you call them?" (this expression was used by respondents who could not remember the word *Alukta*)[129] or *orang kafir* – heathen. All of these derogatory terms reflect the negative and condescending attitude of Christians towards indigenous belief. They show that *Alukta* is not regarded as a religion.

2.3.4.4 The Customary Law Adat, Aluk Todolo and Christianity

It might seem at first glance that the adoption of Christianity in the Toraja region was highly successful and unproblematic, since less than a century after the first Christians entered the territory, 89 % of the population now officially claim the religion. In fact the Toraja might have adopted the new faith, but at the same time, they have preserved their original customs to a great degree and their current faith thus takes on a very specific form. This is most noticeable with the complex funeral rites, which form has been modified only slightly, with the addition of some Christian elements. I believe that if a Christian of non-Toraja origin were to attend a funeral, he or she would never identify this rite as Christian (with the exception of the traditional mass, which now forms an integral part of it).

Particularly at the beginning, religious authorities were at a loss concerning how to convince the adult Toraja to abandon the practice of the *Alukta* and convert to a religion so different from their own autochthonous belief system. The Protestants at first completely rejected everything connected with the indigenous religion, but when this method proved rather ineffective, they eventually refrained from it. The Catholic priests were more cautious; slowly acquainting themselves with Toraja culture, they would then point out to the congregation during mass the spiritual tenets which were in contravention of

---

129 I believe that under the influence of Christianity, which rejected *Alukta,* many Toraja simply banished the word from their minds.

the teachings of the Bible. In spite of this, the indigenous rituals continued to take place almost unaltered. In the latter half of the 20th century priests and pastors thus came up with a bizarre solution: they essentially "divided" the culture into two parts; that is, they interpreted and presented it on two levels. The first of those was *adat*, or customary law, which entails all the practices a dutiful Toraja may perform even after embracing Christianity. These include ancestral traditions, and it was therefore considered advisable to adhere to these and cultivate them. The other level was *Alukta*, that is, the indigenous religion of the ancestors, which had been classified as archaic and in contradiction to the Christian faith, and therefore was to be renounced at every turn. This division gave the Toraja the impression that they were good Toraja Christians, for their rituals observed both the Toraja *adat* (customs) and Christianity.

From the outset of my field research, the Christian funerals indeed seemed to me very similar to the *Alukta* ceremonies as I knew them from the relevant literature. When I expostulated that the sacrifice of buffaloes and pigs during funeral rites was clearly typical of the *Alukta*, it was explained to me that this custom is derived from the *adat,* and as such forms an integral part of Toraja culture. For this reason, buffaloes and pigs are sacrificed even today, when a vast majority of the population is of Christian persuasion. After some time, I started to inquire as to who the arbiter dictating the extant rules actually was. I found that it was the priests and pastors who decided what was allowed and what was forbidden during a given ceremony, but in spite of their efforts, it was evident that the Toraja Christian rituals were still very strongly influenced by the indigenous religion.

2.4 Important Aspects of Toraja Culture

2.4.1 Social Stratification and Its Influence on Society

Another aspect which exerts a strong influence to this day on Toraja rituals is social stratification. In the past, society was strictly divided into several social classes, their number and character depending on the customs of the given locality. This stratification was most pronounced in terms of ruling, the organization of weddings and above all of funerals; according to *Aluk Todolo* it had existed already in heaven.[130] The division of society into four social classes

---

130 According to the creation myth, the first slaves in heaven were *Datu Bakka'* and *Pong Malaleong*. The myth of creation further states that when *Puang Bura' Langi'* descended from heaven to earth, he was accompanied by a slave named *Pong Pako Lando*. See section 2.3.1.

probably occurred after the arrival of the so-called *tomanurun,* the "people descended from heaven" (see section 2.3.1) in the 13th century.

The highest social class, *tana' bulaan* (the golden stake) consisted of the high nobility who were spared all mundane tasks and who, since time immemorial, had enjoyed a multitude of privileges. Unlike the lower orders, they were allowed, for instance, to decorate the carvings on their houses with paint, as well as enjoy the privilege of hosting the most splendid funeral rites, accompanied by vast offerings. It was their mission to ensure the observation and correct interpretation of the customary law of *adat,* as well as to provide for their slaves. The second group, *tana' bassi* (the iron stake) formed the lower nobility. Its members often acted as assistants to the *tana' bulaan* in the resolution of problems related to administration. The third class, *tana' karurung* (the palm stake) were the common freemen who formed a substantial segment of Toraja society, and who worked for the above-named classes. They made a living chiefly as craftsmen. The fourth class, *tana' kua-kua* (the reed stake) was represented by those slaves who had no social rights whatsoever, but a multitude of duties. Marampa'[131] cites a social division into only three groups. According to this analysis, the first category included the members of the highest nobility, the *tana' bulaan* (the golden stake), also referred to as *tokapua* (great people), who formed roughly 10% of the population. The second group included the lower gentry, the *tana' bassi* or *tomakaka* (middle class), representing about 20% of the total population. The third class, *tobuda* (majority society) made up the remaining 70% of the population and consisted of both *tana' karurung* (free people) and *tana' kua-kua* (slaves). In former times, one was either born a slave, or became a slave during one's life. One of the ways a free man could fall into bondage was the inability to pay debts, mostly debts incurred from gambling. Another reason why somebody became enslaved was because he or she was captured by enemies and sold into captivity as a result of the local conflicts during the 19th century.

One could assume that with the adoption of Christianity, the entire class division with its strictly defined rights and duties would have gradually disappeared. I found this problem fascinating and therefore many times asked my respondents to what extent the traditional class identity determined their life even today. Some believed that the class stratification was present only minimally today, while others claimed the very opposite. It is nonetheless certain that some signs of the original stratification manifest themselves in various degrees in the everyday life of the Toraja even in the early 21st century.

Most illuminating regarding a better understanding of this social phenomenon was an interview I conducted in May 2006 with the Catholic

---

131 *Marampa' (Mengenal Toraja),* pp. 42–44.

Priest Lucas Paliling.[132] He stressed that based on differences in customary law, the Toraja region was divided into several areas whereby different sets of rules applied. It is therefore hardly surprising that many respondents answered my question differently. Tallulembangna (nowadays a part of Tana Toraja) consists of three regions – Makale, Sangalla' and Mengkendek, which even today are headed by local rulers using the noble title of *Puang* (God). In the western parts of the Toraja region (nowadays a part of Tana Toraja), the representatives of supreme power are to this day titled *Ma'dika* (Freeman). Surviving social stratification in Tana Toraja is at present still strong, influencing above all the form of their funeral rites (even today the type of ritual an individual must perform is strictly determined according to their class identity). North of Tallulembangna lies what is known as the central part of the Toraja region (the area around Ke'te' Kesu' – nowadays a part of Toraja Utara) where stratification is not as distinct as in Tana Toraja. Marampa' cites that the men of the ruling class are referred to in these parts as *Siambe'* (Noble Father) and the women as *Sindo'* (Noble Mother). To the north from here lies what is at present the most democratic territory, Sa'dan (nowadays a part of Toraja Utara). Class division exists here too, but it is far less visible than in other regions. This circumstance has a major impact on the contemporary form of their funerals. According to Marampa', the noblemen in this area were referred to as *Puang* or *Pong*.[133] In Tallulembangna (Tana Toraja), the funeral ceremonies are more modest in present time. The social strata are absolutely clearly defined here, and thus there is an unambiguous prescription for everyone regarding what sort of funeral they may hold. On the other hand, in Toraja Utara, where class divisions are relatively vague, people hold spectacular funerals in order to "prove" their sense of belonging to a certain social class. Between the declaration of the independent Republic of Indonesia (1945) and the division of Tana Toraja (2008),[134] the vast majority of the government officials in the Toraja region came from the south (nowadays called Tana Toraja). The Toraja from the north and from the Kesu' region (nowadays Toraja Utara) responded to this exclusion from political life by focusing on the support of traditional culture and its preservation.[135] With one sole exception, from 1945 until 2008 the *bupati*[136] in the Toraja region had always

---

132 Unless stated otherwise, all information presented in the following section come from this interview.
133 *Marampa'* (*Mengenal Toraja*), p. 43.
134 As mentioned earlier in section 2.2.4 in the year 2008, the regency of Tana Toraja was divided into Tana Toraja (in the south) and Toraja Utara (in the north).
135 The village of Ke'te' Kesu' has in fact been listed as a UNESCO World Heritage site.
136 *Bupati* (Ind.) – a high government dignitary, the head of the *kabupaten* (administrative subdivision of a province).

hailed from the south.[137] The Toraja from the north who wished to participate in the administration of their region naturally thought it was necessary to change this situation and struggle to break away from the south which they finally did in 2008. A separation was also seen to bring economic advantages – for a tax is paid for every sacrificed animal in the Toraja region, which used to be then divided across the whole territory. Significantly more buffaloes and pigs are sacrificed during grandiose funeral ceremonies in the north than in the south; and thus after the separation, the tax income of the north has been substantially higher than under the previous circumstances, where it used to be re-distributed to the whole of the Toraja region. The Toraja in the south were mostly against separation, one of their main reasons being a fear that this would make it easier for Islam to achieve a foothold in their territory. It is interesting that Father Lucas anticipated the separation already at the time of our interview in the year 2006 mentioning that problems between the north and the south were indeed quite serious and acute at that moment.

2.4.2 The Classification of Rituals

The Toraja themselves as a rule classify their rituals into two main groups. The first of these comprises the *Aluk Rambu Tuka'* (smoke ascending rituals), sometimes also known as *Aluk Rampe Matallo* (rites of the rising sun). These are rituals to secure prosperity on earth for people and their animals as well as their fields. Animals – primarily buffaloes, pigs and roosters, but sometimes others – are slaughtered east of the *tongkonan*, the traditional house, because the east is seen as the direction of life. These sacrifices are accompanied by prayers that appeal to *Puang Matua* (God) and to the deities – *deata*. The *Aluk Rambu Tuka'*, which are always held before noon, include weddings, transition rituals connected to the birth of a child, the cropping of hair, the filing of teeth, rituals performed at the building or reconstruction of a house, and rites such as *merok* (a thanksgiving for happy life), *maro* (to heal the ailing) and *bua'* (celebrating a good harvest).

The second group is called *Aluk Rambu Solo'* (smoke descending rituals), or *Aluk Rampe Matampu'* (rites of the setting sun). These include primarily funerals, and as Nooy-Palm cites,[138] in earlier times also rites connected with

---

137 The sole *bupati* who hailed from the north was shot in his car in the Enrekang region on the way to Makassar. It is believed that his assassination was the work of Toraja from the south, headed by the military leader Ande Sose, a native from the Mengkendek region in the south of the Toraja region.
138 *Nooy-Palm* 1986, p. 3.

head-hunting, which took place when an eminent member of society died.[139] Buffaloes and pigs are sacrificed to the souls of the ancestors, invariably after noon and west of the house, for the south and the west are regarded as the sphere of death. Toraja funeral rites take a variety of forms – from the simplest ones, where the sacrifice of a single egg is sufficient, to the most complex which require several days, where dozens of buffaloes and hundreds of pigs are slaughtered, requiring several months of preparations. The number of animals sacrificed in various types of funerals differs depending on the locality and habits practised there. The family choose a type of ceremony based on the social status of the deceased. Today, however, the financial situation of the family is also taken into account. Before the ritual itself, the family members convene with the mayor or other local authorities in order to determine what sort of funeral will be held, at which date and how many buffaloes will be sacrificed. If the funeral is a more complex affair, it may require several meetings of this kind.

The simplest funeral known as *disilli'* (lit. to be interred) lasts only a few hours and is held for the death of an infant or a very young child. If a baby dies immediately after birth, it is buried together with the placenta without a religious ceremony. If the child was still toothless, its body is deposited in the trunk of a tree in order to gain strength before departing from this world to the realm of spirits. The second option is interring the child in a stone sepulchre. This kind of ceremony is also held for the demise of an adult from the lowest rank, *tana' kua-kua*, someone who had no possessions whatsoever during their life. The costs of such a funeral are absolutely minimal. Formerly the sacrifice on such occasion consisted of a single chicken egg. These days a pig is sometimes sacrificed on the burial site. *Dipasang bongi* (one night) is a ritual lasting one day and one night, following the death of a person who was of the lowest class (*tana' kua-kua*) but actually owned property, or a very poor member of the third class, *tana' karurung*. On such occasions, a pig and a buffalo, or sometimes just a buffalo, is the sacrifice. *Dipatallung bongi* (three nights) lasts three days and nights, with the sacrifice of at least three buffaloes and approximately ten pigs.

Foremost among the more complex rituals is the *dipalimang bongi* (five nights), lasting five days and five nights, with the sacrifice of five buffaloes and dozens of pigs.[140] This type of ceremony may include making a *tau-tau lampa* (bamboo figure) which is then dressed in human clothes, either male or female

---

139 *Tsintjilonis* (2000, pp. 27–28) cites that in earlier times, head hunting expeditions were quite widespread in the mountain areas of South Sulawesi. The Sa'dan practised human sacrifice only for ritual purposes. The custom was not common throughout the whole of the Sa'dan territory but only in some areas.

140 *Sandarupa* 2000, p. 37. *Marampa'* (*Mengenal Toraja*, p. 67) nevertheless cites that during the *dipatallung bongi* four buffaloes must be slaughtered, and with *dipalimang bongi* no less than nine buffaloes.

depending on the gender of the deceased. *Dipapitung bongi* (seven nights) is held for seven days and seven nights. The sacrifice involves often as many as twenty buffaloes (and sometimes even more) and a multitude of pigs, which are slaughtered every day throughout the duration of the ritual. The highest type of funeral, the *rapasan* is comprised of not one, but two ceremonies. In earlier times, these were separated from one another by a period of several months or even years. At present they are more likely to last just a few days. The first of these, *aluk pia* (lit. the child ceremony), is held by the house where the deceased is buried, and the second, *aluk dio rante* (lit. ceremony in the *rante* area), is held in an open area designated for funeral rites – *rante*.[141] In various areas, the *rapasan* fall into sub-categories, with slight modifications in the rules. Still, certain basic features are identical in all of these rituals: the funeral is held twice, and it is an extremely complex and costly affair, which only the wealthy can afford. It involves the sacrifice of dozens of buffaloes of various types, each with a strictly set function within the ritual, and of hundreds of pigs.

2.4.3 The Traditional House

The traditional house – *tongkonan* (lit. the place for sitting) plays an important role in Toraja funeral rites. Apart from its primary function, it is also the place where the deceased "waits" (in some cases for as long as several years) for his or her funeral. According to traditional rules, a newly built house could never be called *tongkonan*. In order to be honoured with this name, it would need to have been inhabited by several successive generations who, over time, had administered a series of adjustments, accompanied by holding the most costly rituals. Only after long years and accomplishing numerous rites would the traditional house be entitled to the name *tongkonan*.

The traditional house which naturally serves as the residence of a family also has a crucial significance in determining the membership within a kin group – *rapu*. Members of the *rapu* are the living descendants of a respected founder (the revered ancestor whose name is always invoked in various rituals) of their shared house, in regard to which they all have certain rights and duties. Given the fact that the Toraja are bilateral, each individual is a member of two groups of descendants – both matrilinear and patrilinear, each deriving their origin from several houses. In reality, the number of these is virtually impossible to establish, but in practice, an individual will generally identify with the houses of his mother, father and the grandparents. After marriage he or she will also

---

141 *Sandarupa* 2000, p. 38.

become a member of all of the *rapu* of his or her partner. Over the course of one's life, one thus becomes a member of several family groups. The prestige of the *tongkonan* depends on its antiquity as well as the social class of its founder.[142] As Waterson cites,[143] most *tongkonans* include a bamboo or coconut grove or even a rice field, which may have been donated to the *tongkonan* by a childless relative. This property is called *mana'* and it should under no circumstances be divided or sold, since it is the property of the *rapu* as a whole. The fields are usually farmed by the family who reside in its house, and keep its proceeds. Sometimes the means thus attained are invested into the repairs of the *tongkonan* or used to finance the school fees of the most gifted children of the *rapu*. In each house, heirlooms are kept – ancient fabrics, daggers, headdresses, adornments such as *kandaure*,[144] and *ambero*[145] (see Figs. 10 and 28) or other artefacts, which, according to tradition, likewise must not be sold. The *tominaa* Tato' Dena' nonetheless told me that today it is relatively common that some relatives purloin these items and sell them. If they then hold a ritual which requires the display or use of these heirlooms, they borrow them from a *tongkonan* which still owns them. The affiliation to a given *tongkonan* is absolutely crucial in the selection of the burial site and partly even the tomb in which the deceased is to be buried, as well as in the repairs of the house and the performance of rituals connected to such an important event.[146] The *tongkonan* had always been, and to a large degree, still remains the site where almost all major rituals are held.

The traditional Toraja house is erected on four tall rectangular pylons, about three metres high (see Fig. 3). It is built of wood and bamboo only, without a single nail or any piece of iron for the joinery. The shape of the saddleback bamboo roof is reminiscent of a ship. Even today it remains unclear why the Toraja build their dwellings in this curious form; nonetheless there exist two theories purporting to explain this phenomenon. According to one, the ancestors of the Toraja sailed to Central Sulawesi from the sea up the Sa'dan River, and having nowhere to stay, they pulled their ships ashore and settled inside them. The other interpretation argues that the peculiar roof of the *tongkonan* represents

---

142 In former times when marriages were allowed only within the same social stratum, all members of a *tongkonan* were of the same class. Today, however, when the social origin of the spouses no longer plays a role, members of a single *rapu* may hail from different social strata.

143 *Waterson* 1995, p. 199.

144 An adornment made of tiny multi-coloured beads. Originally belonging to the *tongkonan*, it is worn by women to beautify the upper part of their body. It can also be placed on a bamboo canopy to decorate a structure which resembles a half-open umbrella.

145 An adornment similar to the *kandaure*, though of different shape, worn by women strapped around the waist.

146 Members of a *tongkonan* naturally have a duty to participate in the ritual concerning the reparation of the house, most often by sacrificing a pig. Their contribution may, however, sometimes be purely symbolic.

the horns of the animal that is most sacred to the Toraja – the buffalo.[147] The tradition of the intricate construction of the *tongkonan* survives to this day, although a majority of the population prefer more comfortable housing. What looks on the outside as a beautiful and spacious abode is in fact rather dark and cramped inside. Every traditional Toraja house is built on a north-south axis, with the front section oriented towards the north, for the Toraja regard the north and the east as the directions of life, as opposed to the west and the south which are connected with death (this fact also plays a role in the practice of rituals).

Placed opposite the house is invariably the *alang* (the granary, sometimes there may be several built in a row – see Fig. 1), very similar in shape to the *tongkonan*. Though it is somewhat smaller, it is strikingly alike in form, as it is also on pylons, which are round and smooth so that mice cannot climb them. The roof of the granary is essentially identical, the carved and painted ornaments adorning its walls are likewise similar. In earlier times the more granaries stood opposite the house, the wealthier and more respective the owner was. Several of these storehouses attached to a house meant that their owner had a rich rice harvest from large fields. To this day the *alang* serves primarily for storing rice, but is also used for seating guests of honour during funeral rites.

Tongkonan is divided horizontally into three floors. The highest section, the attic, is where the sacred family heirlooms are kept, stored in special crimson chests of sandalwood, or in yellow chests made of the wood of the *nangka* tree.[148] The residential middle section is vertically partitioned into three areas.

---

147 To this day, houses with similarly shaped roofs are built by the Batak in North Sumatra, and Minangkabau people of West Sumatra. The cultures of the Toraja, the Batak and the Dayak of Kalimantan display a number of elements in common. The three ethnic groups belong to the first wave of arrivals to the region, known as the Proto-Malay. The roof of the Toraja sarcophagi is a small-scale version of the roof of an actual house and thus even here it is impossible to establish whether its shape is reminiscent of a boat or buffalo horns. The eminent Czech linguist and expert on Indonesia Zorica Dubovská pointed out to me that both the Batak and the Dayak in fact have sarcophagi in the form of boats – the Batak call them *parholian* and they feature the motif of a navigator. She thus surmises that the roofs of the houses of Proto-Malay ethnic groups symbolize ships, essentially a reminiscence of their origin. These cultures believe that their ancestors came to the area they now inhabit on ships, and as they had no houses there, they re-purposed the vessels as dwellings. For the Deutero-Malay – including the above-cited Minangkabau – the roof symbolizes the buffalo horns, the emblem of power and strength. The buffalo is an animal of tremendous significance to the Minangkabau. According to one theory, the term Minangkabau corresponds with the Indonesian phrase *menang kerbau* (*menang* /Ind./ – to win, *kerbau* /Ind./ – buffalo). According to myth, in the era of Majapahit, when the army of Gajah Mada fought in Minangkabau, two ungulate animals were set against one another. The bull for the Javanese, and the buffalo for the Minangkabau – though smaller and weaker, the buffalo's horns were fitted with iron spikes. In the end, the buffalo won and the Minangkabau derive their name from the event. There nonetheless exist other theories explaining the etymology of the term.

148 *Samban, Parinding et al.* 1988, p. 73. The *nangka* tree (*Artocarpus heterophyllus*) is an Asian tropical tree with edible fruit weighing up to 27 kg.

The *tangdo'*, the north room, serves as a bedroom for the grandparents and other adult members of the family (with the exception of the head of family, his wife and their young children) and for guests. It is to the north room that one would retire for saying prayers to the deity. The main central room, *sali,* is placed slightly lower and divided into two areas. The eastern, symbolizing life, is a kitchen (*dapo'*) with a fireplace. It consists of a wooden beam filled with soil, with three flat stones on which pots are placed. The *tongkonan* is not equipped with a chimney – when food is being prepared, the whole house becomes smoky as a result. For this reason it is called *banua merambu* (the house of rising smoke) in Toraja. The kitchen is the exclusive domain of women who are in charge of preparing daily meals. The men, on the other hand, are in charge of preparing the ritual repast that is always cooked outdoors. The westward section of the *sali* is where the deceased is deposited during the funeral.[149] The room may be partitioned by hanging mats into several sections, depending on the current number of sleepers. *Sali* thus serves as kitchen, dining room and bedroom at the same time. The south room, *sumbung,* is the bedroom of the patriarch, his wife and young children. The south, however, symbolizes the sphere of death and the Toraja thus put their dead here until the right time for their burial.[150] The space under the house, *sulluk,* is also called *bala tedong* (buffalo stable), since formerly the buffaloes were kept between the pylons. The Dutch administration banned this practice for hygienic reasons, and the Toraja were thus gradually forced to abandon it.

At present, almost every house is adorned with carved and coloured ornaments on all sides. In earlier times, decorating the entire house was the privilege of noble families, who first had to hold a funeral rite of the highest degree, the *rapasan,* and only then were they allowed to have their house decorated in this manner. The quantity and nature of the ornaments sent an instant message as to who resides in the house. In modern times this custom has been abandoned entirely, and virtually every house that is built today is at the same time adorned with carvings.[151] The north facade had always received special attention, for the Toraja believed that it was in the north that their god *Puang Matua* resided, who would thus look at this side of the house – particularly during the *merauk* ritual (a ritual of thanksgiving to *Puang Matua*) which takes place in front of the house.[152] This side of the house is commonly adorned with a pair of carvings called the *pa'barre allo* representing the sun and its rays, with rooster symbolizing sunrise placed on the sides or above. The gable often features a wooden sculpture

149 *Sandarupa* 1984, p. 22.
150 *Samban, Parinding et al.* 1988, p. 73.
151 *Tominaa* Tato' Dena', April 25, 2006.
152 *Samban, Parinding et al.* 1988, pp. 76–78.

representing the head of a buffalo in life-size, known as *kabongo'*, usually crowned with actual buffalo horns. Another frequent feature is the *katik* – the three-dimensional carving of a long-necked bird, with a hen-like head.[153] The front of the house displays the pride of each family – the horns of the buffaloes sacrificed during rituals. Another favourite motif is the *pa'tedong*, a stylized buffalo head. The carved ornaments which may take the form of geometrical figures, pigs, birds, plants, fruit or celestial bodies always have a religious and symbolic meaning.

Only four colours are used for tinting the carved ornaments – black, white, yellow and red. Black pigment was traditionally extracted from the soot which formed on the bottom of a pot used for cooking over open fire. Today it is manufactured using gasoline and petroleum. Yellow is made by processing yellow clay, and red is made by processing red soil. The production of white tint was rather complex, as it required a multitude of small snails. Their bodies were extracted from shells which would then be dried and burned until they turned white and subsequently ground into a powder containing lime. At present, a far more simple method of burning limestone is used to produce the pigment. Formerly, the yellow, red and white pigments were mixed with palm wine (*tuak*) to make them weatherproof. Today the *tuak* is generally replaced by varnish, or else purely synthetic pigments are used – those are nevertheless not very popular since they fade rather quickly.[154]

According to myth, the colour that preceded all else was black, at a time when there was neither Earth, Heaven, nor the Sun, and the world was a homogeneous mass of blackness. In ancestral tradition the colour thus symbolizes fusion. At last God was born, a ray of light in an otherwise dark universe. That is the origin of white, the symbol of the divinity. Subsequently *Puang Matua* created all else – man, Earth, Moon, the stars and the Sun, and the colour yellow emerged, the emblem of majesty.[155] It is reminiscent of leaves that wither and turn yellow with age. When yellow turmeric is mixed with white limestone, the resulting colour is red, the symbol of valour.[156]

Most dwellings were in earlier days scattered across hillsides. Separate villages – the *tondok* – enclosed with either stone walls or hedges – were independent as a rule, only occasionally forming federations. Where more houses are built in one place, they are aligned in rows next to one another,

---

153 *Nooy-Palm* 1979, pp. 239–240.
154 *Tominaa* Tato' Dena', May 1, 2006.
155 I cite the enumeration of individual features in the same order as listed by *tominaa* Tato' Dena'.
156 *Tominaa* Tato' Dena', April 25, 2006. He further pointed out to me that rice also appears in these four colours. White, red and black rice exist naturally, yellow rice is made by boiling white rice with turmeric (and usually also with coconut milk and other spices).

with rice granaries opposite the *tongkonan* across a pathway. Formerly each village had fields, a bamboo or coconut palm grove and an open area – usually circular – known as *rante*, where funeral rites were held.

2.4.4 Types of Tombs

The house and the grave are often understood as a pair – *sipasang* – the *tongkonan* (house) is not complete unless it has a *liang*, a burial vault (a vault carved in rock – see Fig. 4). Its founder is remembered with as much reverence as the founder of the *tongkonan*. The Toraja not only know where their notable ancestor had come from – they also remember exactly where he is buried. Given the fact that every person is a member of several *tongkonans*, they are entitled to be interred in many *liangs*. As a rule they are buried in the locality where they spent the largest part of their life, or even more often, where they died. However, there are cases when husband and wife wish to be buried together, a request which is nonetheless interpreted as a breach of loyalty to one's own family, for such an individual puts the love for his or her partner above the bonds to their own family. Since it is a person's last wish, however, it is usually complied with. Sometimes the married couple has to establish an entirely new tomb for the purpose. It is remarkable that in some cases the families will quarrel (sometimes going as far as skirmishes) where the departed should be buried. For in the past the Toraja believed that the soul of the departed should feel that both parties produced an effort to win the body of the deceased for their tomb.[157] In earlier times in particular it was extremely important to bury the dead in the right grave, for the body could not be moved at will subsequently. A person buried in the wrong place was known as a *topusa* (lit. a lost person), and the relatives who had caused this blunder provoked much umbrage in the area. Opening the door of the *liang* (tomb), which would enable the transfer of the departed, could only be performed during the *ma' nene'* ritual, which paid homage to the ancestors.[158]

The *liang*, where the members of the upper orders would be buried, particularly in earlier times, is carved in a steep rock and sealed with a small

---

157 *Waterson* 1995, pp. 207–212.

158 The ritual was held approximately once a year, always after the ritual attendant to the rice harvest. On this occasion, a pig would be usually sacrificed in front of the tomb; a new set of clothes was placed next to the deceased, and the *tau-tau* statues garments were also changed. The ritual is still practised today, but rather than viewed as paying respect to the ancestors, it is understood that the duty of the family is to tend to the family grave. *Waterson* (1995, p. 208) cites that the Catholic Church which is generally more open to the elements of *Alukta* in fact went as far as incorporating the *ma'nene'* in the celebrations of the All Saints festivities.

wooden door. It is placed high enough that it can only be reached by ladder. Its construction is a costly affair, as well as time-consuming, and thus it was always the privilege of wealthy noblemen; the less affluent would use crevices in rocks formed by erosion. Several tombs are always found in one rock.

At present the rich descendants of the members of any social class generally use the most modern type of tomb – *patane*. It is a small brick structure, its flat roof often crowned by a small-scale replica of a *tongkonan* roof. The *patane* looks like a little house; in fact it is actually in a better condition than many real dwellings, often placed in a site offering an exquisite view. The rules of burial in a *patane* and in a *liang* are identical.

The first type of graves which appeared in this locality were the so-called hanging graves, the *erong* (see Fig. 5), whose existence dates to a period 800 years ago. The coffins in which the departed were deposited were made of wood in the form of a pig, a buffalo, a ship or a traditional house. They would be suspended under rock overhangs where they were sheltered from the ravages of rain and wild animals. A single coffin would always contain only one family. After some time had elapsed, a body would be reduced to bones, thus providing enough room for other family members. Today the vestiges of the *erong* can be found for instance in Ke'te' Kesu'.

Another type of tomb which is no longer built today is the *pangkaro*. This type of little bamboo house seated on an artificial earth mound was designated solely for the members of the highest caste. Its interior was divided into two parts, the first for the departed and the second for his or her slave. If the slave preceded his master in death, he would be buried in the tomb, where the master would eventually follow. If the master was the first one to die, the clothes of the slave were placed in the grave. When he eventually died, he was buried next to his master.

In locales with the large banyan trees, young children who died while still toothless would most often be buried in the trunk of this tree. This type of grave is termed *liang – pia* (a vault for children).

The small balconies with wooden railing in front of the *liang* tombs frequently feature statues of the departed – *tau-tau* (see Figs. 6 and 7). The departed are carved in life size from the wood of the *nangka* tree or from sandalwood. In the past, these statues could be made only if the funeral was going to last for a minimum of seven days. Like many other old rules, this is not strictly observed today, and it is typically up to the family to make these decisions. If they feel that the funeral is large enough and have enough funds at their disposal, they will simply go ahead and procure the *tau-tau*. Originally the *tau-tau* figures did not reflect the actual demeanour of the departed; only later, after woodcarvers had visited Bali and fallen under the sway of Bali art, did they start to attempt a realistic portrayal of the face of the deceased. At present the *tau-tau* always represent a stylized figure of the departed which is clad in the deceased's clothes; the women are attired in *sarongs*[159] and *kebayas*.[160] The whites of their eyes may be made of bone, or the pupils of buffalo horn. Where rituals lasted five days, the custom was to make a bamboo figure – *tau-tau lampa*. It would also be dressed in men's or women's clothes, but would not be preserved – it was discarded directly after the ceremony. These figurines exist to this day, but to a much lesser degree than in the past.

Nooy-Palm[161] cites that originally in *Aluk Todolo,* the statue represented the departed. Its followers believed that the soul of the deceased dwells in the *tau-tau*. Representatives of Gereja Toraja (the Toraja Protestant Church)[162] were therefore against the use of these figurines at Christian funerals. Matters went so far that in 1983, there was actually a major conflict between representatives of the church and wealthy Toraja Christians. The latter differed from the opinion of the church representatives, insisting emphatically that souls do not dwell in the *tau-tau*. In their understanding, the statue was no more than a sort of portrait of the departed, and above all, a symbol of his or her social status. Several Christians in fact voiced the opinion to me that although in earlier times people believed that the soul of the departed resides in the *tau-tau*, today the statue is regarded merely as an artistic portrayal of the deceased. In general it can be said that as far as upper-class Christian burials are concerned, the use of *tau-tau* is more frequent among Catholics. Unlike the Catholic Church, the Protestant Church actually bans their use in practice.

2.4.5 The Buffalo – The Most Important Animal in Toraja Culture

The water buffalo (*Bos bubalus /var. sondaica/*),[163] called the *tedong* or *karembau* in Toraja – however, the latter is a poetic term used only in prayers,[164] is unequivocally regarded in Toraja culture as the most important of all animals. Buffaloes are not only present at various rituals, they also have a unique role

---

159 *Sarong* (Ind.) – a broad strip of fabric, the ends of which are sewn together. It is worn wrapped around the loins, covering the lower part of one's body. The garment, similar to a skirt, is worn by both men and women, both as casual wear and during festive occasions.
160 *Kebaya* (Ind.) – a women's garment similar to a blouse.
161 *Nooy-Palm* 1986, p. 170.
162 Gereja Toraja is a church drawing on the doctrines of the Gereformeerde Zendings Bond, whose missionaries were the first Christians on the territory of present-day Tana Toraja and Toraja Utara. From 1947 the Gereja Toraja has been an independent church.
163 *Nooy-Palm* 1979, p. 184.
164 *Nooy-Palm* 2003, p. 96.

in the social and economic spheres. Furthermore, the image of the buffalo is an important motif in Toraja art. These most prized of all animals are an essential part of every important ritual, so as a result, there is a shortage of water buffaloes, and they have to be imported by traders from other areas.

Buffaloes are so popular that they in fact represent a frequent subject of everyday conversation among local men. Nooy-Palm goes so far as to say: "People talk about buffaloes with the fervor of Europeans discussing pedigree dogs."[165] My own first-hand observation likewise leads me to the conclusion that the Toraja show towards buffaloes the same love that Europeans demonstrate towards their pets. Since ancient times, buffaloes have been looked after by *gembala* (shepherds) aged ten to eighteen.[166] The task of these boys is to lead the buffalo to pasture, wash it in the river, and provide it with general care. Almost daily, they clean its hide with a brush, as well as polish both its hooves and horns. After the buffalo is killed, its hide passes to its shepherd. Often, they sell it on the spot to adults, who then sell it at market for up to five times the price (in 2002 this amounted to approx. 10 US dollars). Buffaloes are cherished to such a degree that they are not used as plough animals, as is commonly done in Java or Bali. If the Toraja use them for field work, they generally choose animals regarded as the least comely, typically the female cows of the species. In most rituals, only males are sacrificed, for they are larger in body, and their horns are more spectacular. With pigs and poultry, the same preference prevails.

The buffalo, according to mythology of celestial origin,[167] plays an important role in many areas of Toraja culture. The deceased, for instance, is regarded as still alive and is referred to as ill – *to makula'* (lit. "hot person") until the moment when the first buffalo is slaughtered during the funeral rite. Only from that point on is a person truly regarded as dead – *to mate* (lit. the dead one). In the past, buffaloes were accorded crucial importance in funeral rites, for the Toraja believed that the souls of the sacrificed buffaloes would escort the soul of the departed to *puya* (see section 3.2.1). The buffaloes also play a major role in the allocation of inheritance. According to the number of animals sacrificed during the funeral of the deceased, the bereaved are allocated a corresponding part of the inheritance. In the old days buffaloes also represented a means of payment. They were indispensable in the case of a divorce, for before the marriage took place, it was established – depending on the social class of the partners – how

---

165 *Nooy-Palm* 1979, p. 184.

166 *Tominaa* Tato' Dena', May 2006. *Nooy-Palm* (1979, p. 190) cites the fact that shepherds are mostly boys aged six to twelve. Due to mandatory school attendance, this task has become much more challenging, caused by the time constraints of juggling both shepherding and their studies.

167 According to myth, the ancestor of the buffalo (*Manturini*) was created by *Puang Matua* (God) in Heaven. See section 2.3.1 and the Genealogy of the Gods no. 3.

many buffaloes would have to be paid in compensation by the partner who caused the break-up of the marriage.

In the visual arts, buffaloes usually have a ritual function. A wooden sculpture representing a life-size buffalo head called a *kabongo'* appears on the gable walls of houses or granaries; another frequently used feature is the stylized buffalo head known as a *pa'tedong*, usually carved on the house or granary door. Both the *kabongo'* and *pa'tedong* have a protective role, as these are meant to prevent evil powers from entering.[168] The sacred cloths which are exhibited during a ritual celebrating a successful harvest – the *bua'* – features buffalo cows with calves, symbolizing fertility.[169] Boys mould buffalo heads with large horns, or even whole figures, out of clay,[170] and young children play with the hooves of freshly slaughtered buffalo, tying them to pieces of string and pulling them around. The magic stone *balo'* which feature in buffalo fights – *ma'pasilaga tedong* – may also be fashioned in the shape of buffalo horns or bodies. The buffalo, as a symbol of the Toraja region, also often appears in fairy tales, parables, proverbs, or folklore.

There is a whole range of criteria according to which buffaloes are classified. Among the most important in particular are the colour of the hide, the type and size of the horns, and their general constitution. The assessment may differ locally. One of the possible forms of classification is based on the colour of their skin.[171] A piebald buffalo with irregularly placed black and white patches is called *tedong bonga*.[172] This group also includes the *tedong saleko*, whose entire body is covered in numerous black and white patches. The *saleko* buffalo is unique and is thus regarded as the most valuable by the Toraja. An adult animal, with a well-developed body and long, firm horns, can be exchanged for up to ten or more common black buffalo.[173] A buffalo called *tedong bonga ulu* is defined by means of the contrast between its white head and its black body and neck. If white also appears on the animal's forehead, it is referred to as *tedong bonga sori* or also *tedong bonga rori'*. The *bonga tengnge'* buffalo[174] is characterized

---

168 *Nooy-Palm* 1979, pp. 193–194.

169 *Nooy-Palm* 2003, p. 109.

170 I witnessed a scene where boys passed the time with this entertainment during a long-winded speech at a funeral. As soon as they realized I was videotaping them, they started competing with each other and producing ever more remarkable creations. *Nooy-Palm* (1979, pp. 194–195) also mentions this phenomenon and in fact says that not only children but grown men also engage in this pursuit, for it is an amusement which is not determined by age.

171 Unless cited otherwise, I draw this information above all from *Nooy-Palm* (1979, pp. 184–189).

172 *Nooy-Palm* (1979, p. 185) cites that the *tedong bonga* has the value of ten to twenty strong black buffaloes.

173 I learned this piece of information at the buffalo and pig market in Bolu, where I spoke to cattle traders.

174 *Tengnge'* (Tor.) – a kind of large bird, whose feathers are of reddish hue, apart from the head and neck.

by a white head and part of the neck, the *tedong todi'* has a white stripe on its forehead. A shared trait of all of these buffaloes is a white tail, or at least the tip of the tail. An animal with a black tail cannot be used for sacrifice. A most rare and thus very costly buffalo is the *tedong lotong boko'*, whose entire body is white, apart from a black back. Another type of buffalo is the *tedong pudu'*, whose hide is dark black, with only its rump of a lighter tone. If a black buffalo has white feet, it is called *tedong suppak* or *tedong ma' kallang*. Of little value is the ashen-grey coloured buffalo known as *tedong sambao'*. The *tedong bulaan* (lit. golden) buffalo is entirely white; it must never be sacrificed during funereal rites and in most areas it is prohibited to partake of its flesh.[175] A neutered buffalo is called *tedong balian*.

The following classification is based on the differences in buffalo horns. *Tanduk sokko* (lit. with the horns coiled downwards) are always pointed downwards, symbolizing respect and courtesy. If the horns almost touch, symbolizing decency and the receiving of a divine blessing, they are referred to as *tanduk sokko mantarima* (lit. horns coiling downwards, which may receive). *Tanduk tarangga* (lit. horns coiled upwards) grow backwards and up, and are crescent-shaped. Buffaloes with this shape of horn are believed to be endowed with courage. *Tanduk pampang* (lit. wide horns) grow to the sides and are relatively long, with a very wide span. It is said that the animals with *tanduk pampang* have the ability to unify. In a funeral procession, the animals walking at the front are always those with *sokko* horns, followed by those with *tarangga* horns, with the procession closing with buffalo with *pampang* horns. There exist two more types of horns – *tanduk sikki'* (lit. horns that coil excessively), which are similar to the *tarangga* horns, but with their ends nearly touching; and also *tanduk tekken langi'* horns where one horn is pointed upwards and the other downwards.[176]

Another classification reflects the length of the horns. Part of an adult (human) male hand is used as the unit of measurement. Thus the horns can be for example as long as the last phalanx of a middle finger, as its two phalanxes, as one finger, as a palm, or as the distance between the tip of the finger and the elbow.[177] Naturally the longer the horns, the more valuable the animal, and the higher its market price. In establishing the latter, the key factors are the aforementioned characteristics, such as the colour of the hide, the type and

---

175 *Nooy-Palm* (1979, p. 155) cites the fact that according to mythology, this buffalo helped a hero named *Polo Padang*, who in returned promised that his progeny would not consume meat from this type of buffalo.

176 The information regarding the classification of the buffalo based on the type of horn was furnished by another informant, the Catholic Priest John Manta, on May 5, 2006.

177 I learned this in conversation with men at the buffalo market.

size of the horns as well as their symmetry, and the general constitution of the body, as well as other characteristics. As a rule, the most expensive is the unique *saleko* buffalo, whose price in 2006 amounted to 10,000 US dollars. A common black buffalo cost roughly 1,000 US dollars, and the price of the remainder fell between these two poles.[178]

An essential part of a large funeral are buffalo fights – *ma'pasilaga tedong*,[179] which were formerly held only during those funerals which lasted five or more days. However, as *tominaa* Tato' Dena' noted with disapproval, today they are held at any funeral where a large amount of buffaloes is sacrificed. The pair of animals selected for a fight are always of similar physique,[180] as they should not be too young (eight years is regarded as the ideal age), with the animals being strong and with long horns. Most buffaloes today are bred in stables, and when outdoors, are always kept under the supervision of a shepherd, who takes them to the river every two or three days. After bathing the buffaloes are made to dry in the sun, in order to get used to its glare so as to be resistant to it during fights. Before the fight, the owner of the buffalo may put the magic stone *balo'* in the pail of water or palm wine *tuak* from which the animal will drink. Its special powers will endow the animal with supernatural strength and probably cause it to win the upcoming fight. *Tominaa* Tato' Dena' showed me the *balo'*, which is a small black (it can be also brown) stone which fits into the palm of a grown man; its shape is reminiscent of a buffalo head with horns. The *balo'* has not been worked into that shape by man, but is always a natural formation. It is kept in the upper part of the house, together with hereditary family relics, and passed down from one generation to another together with other artefacts. It is kept in a cloth pouch, and when it is not being used for ritual purposes it must not be exposed to light for long, as it would otherwise lose its magic powers. Buffalo fights are planned in advance, and thus the day and hour are precisely established. This amusement, naturally accompanied by betting, is the privilege of men. Each time I witnessed the *ma'pasilaga tedong* fights, only men were present at the scene, and not afraid to stand precariously close to the large animals. The fights take place on an open space near the funeral, often surrounded by irrigated rice fields (*sawah*) where the defeated animal as a rule escapes. The fight almost never ends in the death of either of the buffaloes, but

---

178 For comparison: the average salary of a university professor in 2006 was approx. 150 US dollars per month.

179 *Tominaa* Tato' Dena', May 1, 2006.

180 A buffalo trader at the market in Bolu told me that all buffaloes are first sorted into pairs by type, naturally with regard to the physique of each animal. Initially, pairs are formed with buffaloes of the same hue, so that the first fight is between, say, two black animals, followed by two piebald. The winners from the initial round then clash in the next, thus the subsequent pairs of combatants are mixed.

nonetheless both animals are almost invariably sacrificed at the funeral during the following days.

The part called *The Foundations of Toraja Culture* divided into three chapters – *Tana Toraja and Its Inhabitants, The Autochthonous Religion Aluk Todolo and the Adoption of Christianity,* and *Important Aspects of Toraja Culture* provided an introduction into the Tojara region, its inhabitants, and their indigenous religion as well as key aspects of their culture, which influence to a large degree the nature of the most important Toraja ritual today – the funeral.

3 Forms of Funeral Rituals in the Past and Today

3.1 Overview

The following part forms the core of the present work and is based chiefly on the results of my field research. The first chapter discusses what happens to the soul of the departed, according to the indigenous religion *Aluk Todolo*, as well as how the family deals with the body, and to what extent social origin influences the type and duration of the funeral rite even today. There follows an account of an actual Catholic funeral, that of Yohana Maria Sumbung, and an explanation of the shift in the meaning of certain operations as practised by the Christians. The next two chapters record the views of the Toraja adherents of the Pentecostal movement and also of Muslims regarding the current form of funerals.

3.2 General Information on Funeral Rites

Only a few rites display such a variety of forms, dependent on ethnic identity, social class and status, religious confession, age, and sometimes the gender of the departed, as do funeral rites. In many cultures, the rites connected with death are more elaborate than any other ritual, something that is especially true for the Toraja, whose culture is defined by a strong cult of ancestors. Funerals have always ranked as the most important rituals of all with the Toraja, and they have retained their central role to this day. The privileged status of funerals is due to the fact that by performing the correct ritual, the soul of the deceased will reach its destination (*puya*, the realm of souls – see section 3.2.1) where it will be happy and therefore have no need to intervene unfavourably in the lives of relatives. According to the traditional belief *Aluk Todolo*, there existed an unequivocal mutual relationship between the soul of the deceased and the bereaved family. Christians today no longer believe in these correlations, but even so, they continue to organize and perform elaborate funeral rituals.

3.2.1 The Soul After Death

Followers of *Aluk Todolo* believe that after death, a man's soul may live in one of three places, depending on his or her social origin and the rituals performed (involving the sacrifice of buffaloes and pigs): among the living in the human world; in *puya,* the realm of souls, as the soul of the ancestors *To Membali Puang;* or in heaven as one of the deities known as *deata*. It was believed in *Aluk Todolo* that the souls of those for whom no animal was sacrificed would continue to wander the world, pestering the living until one of the relatives finds at least one sacrificial animal. There is in fact a saying in Toraja: *Tae'na ma'din dolamun punti tu to mate* (Everyone must be buried with the performance of sacrifice).[181] *Tominaa* Tato' Dena' told me, however, that if the family of the deceased has no money at all, it is not in fact in contradiction to the *Aluk Todolo* philosophy to simply wash the deceased, dress him, wrap him in a mat and bury him in a crevice in a rock created by erosion.

After a proper funeral rite held in the earthly world *lino,* most of the souls will subsequently enter *puya,* the realm of souls situated in the south. This sphere of death is apparently a place where all problems and diseases vanish. Nooy-Palm cites that it is located south-west of the Toraja region, between Kalosi and Enrekang, and that after performing the funeral rites, human souls reach that place via a hole or tunnel in the ground.[182] The Toraja believed that the human souls reach this afterworld through the souls of sacrificed animals, and it is for this reason that buffaloes and pigs are slaughtered at their funerals. The journey to *puya* was regarded as long and arduous; it was believed that the soul faces various ordeals during its peregrination. For this reason it was necessary to provide well for the deceased. The Toraja formerly believed that the more animals were sacrificed, the larger the number of animal spirits would accompany the soul of their relative, therefore making the pilgrimage to the other world easier. The dead were frequently provided with practical objects,

---

181 *Paranoan* 1994, p. 19.
182 *Nooy-Palm* 1979, pp. 112–113.

such as the cloth in which his or her body was wrapped, various valuables, as well as cups, plates, cigarettes, betel, and other things which they may have favoured in their lifetime. In the old days, it was a matter of great importance for the Toraja to hold a ceremony which would follow all the established rules for the funeral of a member of a given social group. Holding the funeral with all due requisites simultaneously confirmed the class status of the departed. This was very important, for apart from material possessions, the deceased also took with them to *puya* their status. Given the powerful cult of the ancestors, in their notion of life and death the adherents of *Aluk Todolo* saw a clear link between a quiet life on earth and the happiness of the soul after death. By performing the necessary ritual, the bereaved family secured for themselves safety, happiness and prosperity on earth. If, however, the relatives neglected their duty, they believed that they would be plagued thereafter by misfortune. Another condition for the happiness of the soul was the completion of three fundamental tasks during one's lifetime. Each person was to create a descendant, breed farm animals, and farm their land, as reflected in traditional Toraja poetry:

1. To naindanriki' lino
   To natimbayo-bayo
   Lolo' ri Puya
   Inan tontong sae lako

   We are here but temporarily
   We are the shadows of the world
   It is in *Puya*, the realm of souls,
   That is our place for eternity

2. Tang kuriamo medalle
   Sola mekutu padang
   Kukua angku mellolok
   Angku mengkala' rambu tiku

   I am trying to make a living
   To be able to spawn children
     and grandchildren
   Rich, famous, remembered
   My memory kept alive in the heart
     of every man[183]

---

183 *Paranoan* 1994, p. 12. Translation from Indonesian by the author.

According to the *tominaa* Tato' Dena', it is said that in *puya* we shall meet our ancestors, who live a very similar life to ours on earth, except that they are more accomplished than earthly creatures and therefore never err.[184] This statement corresponds to Van Gennep, who claims that although the notion of various ethnic groups regarding the realm of the dead takes different forms, it still always remains similar to the reality of the living, except that life in the nether world is as a rule more pleasant.[185] According to the *tominaa*, it is impossible to cook in *puya* as there are no fires, and so the ancestors wait for their descendants on earth to hold a ritual so they can eat.

According to *Aluk Todolo* only the souls of rich individuals of noble origin ascend to heaven. The highest nobility endowed with the title *Puang* (God) proceed from the world of men directly to heaven without visiting *puya*. The souls of other noblemen depart first to *puya* and only from there proceed to heaven. This is nonetheless possible only if these people had performed the supreme *rambu tuka'* ritual – the ceremony *bua' kassale,* while they were living, and at the same time, their children had held the highest funeral rite, the *rapasan*. The *rapasan* purifies the soul which then proceeds further from *puya*, eventually ascending the Bamba Puang mountain, and from there rising to the firmament to become one of the *deata* (deity).[186]

3.2.2 Providing for the Body After Death

According to *Aluk Todolo*, the soul of the deceased could set forth on the journey to *puya* only after the sacrificing of the first animal, for only with the ritual *makaru'dusan* would the deceased be proclaimed dead, and from that moment on were referred to as *to mate*. Until then, they are only regarded as ill, or *to makula'*. Their relatives treat them accordingly, bringing the deceased food and drink several times a day, and sometimes also cigarettes or betel. Although modern Toraja Christians do not like to admit to this fact, even today, they continue to offer their dead at least symbolic helpings of food at least once a day.

The Toraja region lies in the tropics. In spite of this, the period between death and burial is at least several days, and often as long as several months or years. As a consequence, the body must be washed and mummified immediately

---

184 Tato' Dena' stressed several times that he cannot know whether the information regarding *puya* he furnished me with was authentic. He said it was difficult to speak of the place not having died yet.

185 *Van Gennep* 1997, p. 142.

186 *Dubovská* (1973, p. 169) cites that according to Toraja legend, the souls of the departed sail across the sea back to the original homeland of their ancestors. This notion occurs also with other ethnic groups that have not been under the influence of either Hinduism or Islam.

after death. The medium used most commonly today is formalin,[187] after the application of which the body becomes solid and desiccated. In this form, in a consistency similar to that of wood, the body can be preserved for a period of many years. Formalin is injected into all parts of the body, particularly those most susceptible to decay (eyes, face, mouth, and the abdominal cavity). In this manner, all bacteria are eradicated, accelerating the process of dehydration and preservation. Approximately 600 cm^3 of formalin is needed for the conservation of a body. This manner of mummification began to be practised by the Toraja only in the late 1960s.[188] Before then, bodies were conserved using traditional methods; the person in charge of preservation was called *to mangalai bosi* (lit. the man who removes odour). Mummification was performed with the mixture of the essence of the bud of the areca nut palm, citrus leaves, and the leaves of the *jambu batu* tree.[189] These three ingredients were mixed and soaked in water. After being washed, the body of the deceased would be daubed with this solution, while special prayers were read. This preserved the body and prevented it from decomposing. Mango leaves were used to remove the stench and keep flies from the body; one would be placed on the body of the departed, another would be placed under the house. Sometimes the *to mangalai bosi* would catch the liquid issuing from the nose of the deceased during the washing process in a bamboo stalk, in order to reduce the scent of decay. The bamboo would then be deposited under a tree far from the village, so that the pungent smell would not reach it. A person titled *to ma'peulli'* helped keep the body in good condition; his task was to collect the worms that crawled from it. Ghozi Badrie cites that according to one account, he would then put them back in, and according to another, he would collect them in a bamboo which he would dispose of each night. Another person administering to the dead was *to ma'pemali*, whose task was to oversee that no ritual law set by *Aluk Todolo* was violated.[190] (At present the body is mummified by the relatives; however, if one dies in hospital, the task can be performed by the medical staff, for a fee.) After conservation, the departed would be dressed in ceremonial attire and adorned with the jewellery and accessories that he or she wore in life. After this, the body would be wrapped in a special fabric, *pa'tannun,* woven from the fibres of the green thorns of the pineapple (*pondan datu*). This task was entrusted to the *to mebalun* (the person who wraps). Finally, the body would be placed on a bamboo construction and carried to the south section of the house, called the *sumbung,* where it remained until the commencement of the funeral. For the period which the departed

---

187 Formalin is a compound of formaldehyde and water, in the ratio 4:6.
188 *Ghozi Badrie* 1997, p. 103.
189 *Psidium guajava* – guava fruit tree, from the myrtle family.
190 *Ghozi Badrie* 1997, pp. 48–49 and 102.

was laid in the house, a *to ma'parandan* (man who prepares) kept him or her company; this was always a close relative – the wife, husband, or child. The body of the departed would lie in the same position as the sleeping family members who shared the room with the deceased. The head was turned to the west while the feet pointed to the south, for this direction was considered to be the lifeline by the Toraja. The dead would remain in this position until the moment when he or she was carried to the room called *sali*, proclaimed dead, and placed so that the head would point to the south, regarded as the zone of death, with the feet pointing to the north. Even today, the dead are placed in the house, but the family no longer has a duty to keep them constant company. Yet most families still observe the custom at least partially, and each night one of the family or neighbours sleeps with the body.

Some of these traditions are kept to this day, as I was able to personally ascertain in the course of my field study when I took part in the preparations and subsequently, the funeral of the mother of my informant – Father Stanis, a Catholic priest. During the four-month long preparations, I made several visits to the modern one-story house of his family in Kalolu, where departed Yohana Maria Sumbung was deposited for a period of almost eighteen months before the commencement of the funeral. The room where she was laid at first glance evinced the coexistence of two worlds: the Christian and the Toraja. The dead woman rested in an open coffin (the lid was placed next to her) covered with a transparent light-coloured fabric. She was clad in a long white dress, shoes and gloves, with accessories – glasses, earrings and beads, a rosary clasped in her hands and a bouquet of artificial flowers placed on her stomach. A small low table stood next to the coffin, with a Christian cross erect in a bowl of sand with candles and a pair of rosaries to each side. A Bible, other religious volumes, and a picture of Jesus Christ were laid on the floor. The Christian atmosphere was further evoked by a photograph of the departed and several baskets of artificial flowers placed around her head. Other decorations were unequivocal references to Toraja culture. The walls and ceiling were covered in red fabric, in some places with narrow strips of light-brown cloth featuring a variety of geometric figures and Toraja symbols, as well as motifs of everyday life. These depicted human figures leading buffaloes, warriors, or men carrying pigs on bamboo stretchers. In one place, the fabric formed a crucifix. The walls were further adorned with the traditional daggers, the *gayang*, bead ornaments, the *kandaure* and *ambero*, arranged in a shape reminiscent of the sun. The fusion of Toraja and Christian cultures was also reflected by the fact that even though the family was one of the first to convert to Catholicism, the departed was placed with her head pointing to the west, as is the custom among followers of *Alukta*.

3.2.3 The Role of the Social Status of the Deceased and the Financial Situation of the Family Regarding the Character and Duration of the Funeral

Although death never represented the final end to the Toraja, as it was seen as a transition from one state of being to another, it was nevertheless far from easy to come to terms with it. The period of mourning, the preparation of the funeral and the funeral rite itself granted the family of the departed the time necessary to reconcile themselves with this fact. In the old days, the Toraja used to say that if the deceased was buried immediately after death, such a situation would be for the bereaved as if a hawk careened suddenly upon its prey, snatching it in its talons and vanishing forever in the split of a second. The character and duration of a funeral always corresponded with the social status of the deceased, a practice which to some degree survives to this day. Unlike in the past, however, the financial standing of the family plays a significant role today, alongside social status. A smaller funeral will generally take place several days or weeks after death; larger funerals, however, are held after an interval ranging from several months to several years. The main reason for this is the fact that the surviving members of the family need time for the preparation of the elaborate funeral rite. This time is needed to collect the finances, notify the relatives and procure the items necessary for the funeral rite. A longer interval of time between death and the funeral thus indicates that the departed was a member of higher class and that the funeral will be a lavish affair. However, if a family cannot afford to hold a funeral of magnificence corresponding to the status of the deceased, they do try to speed things along, for a modest ritual held a long time after death would be seen as humiliating.

This was confirmed by an interview with Juchri Layuksugi, whose father, Marthen Mala Layuksugi, died on February 8, 2006, in Makassar. His funeral was, in Toraja terms, held very soon after that – between February 17–19, 2006.

Interview no. 4

J. L.:[191] As for my father, it was three days *(in my father's case the meeting*[192] *took place three days before the start of the funeral)*. Since it was rather sudden, I mean we were in a hurry, we had the meeting three days before the start of the ceremony.

M. B.: Why were you in a hurry? Why did you want to bury him quickly?

J. L.: You see, we wanted to bury him quickly because father died in Makassar,

---

191 Juchri Layuksugi.
192 A meeting where issues related to the upcoming funeral are planned.

or in other words, Ujung Pandang,[193] and we already prayed there according to our faith – Protestantism. My father, or the departed, was registered in Makassar as a member of the Toraja Protestant Church. He was a Protestant and the ceremony was already done in Makassar, all that remained was for the body to be taken from there to Tana Toraja. Also, we happen to have a relative, who is a bound man *(he is employed)*, meaning he works for the government sector, so he cannot go on leave whenever he wants to, and thus he is not free as he is bound to the government, so that was another reason. And secondly, to be honest, I have to admit that it was also because of… well… the financial situation, that's how it is. [*I very much appreciated that the informant imparted to me the true reason for precipitating the funeral, although his choice of words, frequent hesitation and the tone of his voice clearly betrayed that it was not easy for him to admit to this fact.*] For the longer the deceased stays in the house,[194] the greater the expense, so we did it as quickly as possible, well, as I said before, because of our limited finances, to be quite honest. Even though in reality we could have buried Father many days later, if we had so wished, that was not the problem, the real reason was – well, economic difficulties [*Here my respondent expressed the fact that his father had been a member of a higher class, and his funeral thus could have lasted several days longer, and taken place with an interval of several months or even years. However, due to the limited financial means of the family it took place nine days after the father's death, and lasted only three days.*] We made it sooner rather than later, because we had already spent a lot of money in Makassar. How could we then make a long delay of the funeral in Toraja? That would have been an even greater financial strain.

It clearly transpires from the interview that the son felt guilty for the family being unable to provide a larger funeral to correspond to the social origin of the deceased. During the ceremony, I knew that seven buffaloes were sacrificed, but I was unsure of the number of pigs.

Interview no. 5

M. B.: How many pigs were sacrificed, approximately?
J. L.:[195] Well, I actually cannot… *(count)*… If you would… I have that book of records with me, it's all written there…[196]

---

193 In the years 1971–1999 Makassar was officially called Ujung Pandang.
194 The expression "up in the house" is carried over from the time when all Toraja houses were built on pylons.
195 Juchri Layuksugi.
196 Files are kept on the exact number of animals sacrificed during every funeral for tax reasons.

M. B.: Well, approximately?

J. L.: Because it wasn't very… there were not many, you see we had to consider…
    well the economic factor, waste *(it's a waste)*… [*There elapsed a few seconds of
    complete silence.*] Around fifty.

M. B.: That's a lot, fifty, that really is a lot.

Both the respondent's words and countenance clearly showed that he felt
ashamed, and that it was embarrassing for him to talk about this matter. At
present, the reverse situation is common, where the descendants of slaves or
members of the lower classes have attained sufficient wealth to hold a funeral
worthy of a nobleman. Many of them have left the Toraja region, making their
fortunes for example by working for multinational mining corporations, or at
the oil refineries in Kalimantan, or by becoming successful lawyers, doctors, and
engineers, working mostly in Java. Although they have the financial backing,
according to ancestral rules, surviving in large part to this day, they do not
have the right to a sumptuous ceremony. There is no universal solution for such
an eventuality, and each case is assessed individually. Among the determining
factors are the specific area of the Toraja region where the funeral is to be held,
as well as the verdict of the local authorities responsible for organizing the
funeral.[197] When a family wants to perform a ritual that they are not entitled to
according to ancestral rules due to the social class of the departed, the situation
is often resolved by compromise. The family of the deceased are allowed to
slaughter more buffaloes and pigs than their ancestry allows, but have to
observe the number of days prescribed to their class. It also happens that
wealthy individuals hailing from the lower classes do not even strive for having
a sumptuous ceremony, as they realize that their pretensions would make them
the laughing stock of the whole community.

It can thus be said that the funeral rites of the Toraja serve on the one hand
for the cementing and upholding of social status and the class system, and on the
other as a tool of augmenting social prestige. According to some respondents,
the members of the upper classes are now poorer than in earlier times, for the
sums that must be spent on observing rites keep going up. To some extent,
they are also compelled to compete with members of the lower classes who try
to measure up to them in this respect. A situation where noblemen do not have
enough funds to hold costly rituals, and the underclass, on the contrary, have
the requisite means but not the permission to have large funerals may become

---

197 As I have already laid out, the influence of social stratification persists more strongly in the
    south of the Toraja region (in area of the Tallulembangna – Tana Toraja) and thus it is less
    permissible for members of the lower classes to have a large funeral here than it is the north, in
    the Sa'dan region (Toraja Utara).

a potential source of conflict. It happens very often that noblemen endowed with lands but lacking sufficient funds, and worried that their reputation would suffer by holding a less costly ceremony, borrow a buffalo from a member of the lower class, pledging their land as security. Until the time the nobleman returns the buffalo, the lands are farmed and harvested by their temporary holder. The crops thus attained in fact form a sort of "interest" on the lease of the animal. This system has been in place for decades now and has suited both parties well. At present, however, it appears that as a result of numerous social changes, it will soon vanish, which may, to some extent, jeopardize the funerals of less well-off noblemen. Since time immemorial, fields were owned jointly by several relatives, presenting another reason why it could not be sold, as each individual owned it only in part. It was customary for co-owners to give their consent in the event that one of the relatives needed to pawn the field, as they knew they could themselves get into a similar predicament. At present, however, lands are often divided into separate plots and owners may dispose of them as they wish or need. Unlike in the past, the new temporary holder gets only a section of the field, thus reducing the yield. For the middle class, it is becoming more advantageous to keep their money in the bank than to invest it in the purchase and lease of a buffalo, for this modern-day institution enables them to retrieve their finances at will, with an interest that moreover does not require any effort.

The attitude of family members towards funerals generally differs depending on the place of residence. Those who live in the Toraja region mostly persist in the sacrificing of a multitude of animals, with the ceremony including as many traditional features as possible – these nonetheless in their interpretation do not go against the grain of Christianity. Although many would be loath to admit it, having a lavish funeral is a matter of prestige, guaranteeing the respect of the whole community. The Toraja living outside of the Toraja region on the contrary mostly aim to reduce the number of animals sacrificed to the bare minimum. Since they reside outside the area, they are not as concerned about local social standing. On the other hand, it is clear that Toraja rituals can actually exist at such a scale precisely due to their extensive financial support. A grand funeral is a priority for the Toraja, and therefore most of them do not hesitate to spend all of their finances on an opulent ceremony for their closest family members. They invariably justify this behaviour by their "Toraja identity". In this context, it came as a surprise when during one of our conversations the *tominaa* Tato', Dena' soberly observed that people should be prudent with their money and not spend it all on funerals.

Interview no. 6

M. B.: Do you think it is right to spend so much money on funerals?

T. D.:[198] It's usually like this; one should not fritter the property away. It has many uses, many purposes, let us use it for development. In the modern world no less, with the expenses for the children, you can start a business, buy a field, and do other things. You can even farm the land that is still free in the trans areas.[199] So that is good, isn't it? To have capital for a business, for education, for trade and others, one can start a project and do other things.

It is paradoxical for a follower of *Aluk Todolo* to have a more rational approach to the arrangement of funerals than modern Toraja Christians, for whom having an opulent funeral is more than anything a matter of prestige.

3.2.4 The Site of the Funeral Rite and Attendant Rituals

The funeral always takes place in the vicinity of the house of the deceased's family, with greater funerals also in the *rante*, a village common; today, though, it is often in private land immediately adjoining the house that the ceremony is held. Although each space has its specific features, some attributes nonetheless cannot be missing. In the case of a smaller funeral, bamboo stands for guests are installed around the house, adorned with a cloth with Toraja motifs. The preparation of ritual arrangements for a member of the nobility are far more demanding. A wooden tower, *lakkian*, is erected on the funeral site, upon which the coffin with the departed rests for the several days duration of the ceremony. After the funeral, the tower must not be demolished – it must be kept in place until it disintegrates over time.

Other indispensable structures include stands for welcoming guests, and a platform for seating them. All of these sheltered constructions are made of

---

198 Tato' Dena'.
199 What the *tominaa* means by the expression "trans regions" are the areas connected with the transmigration program. This measure had already been introduced at the beginning of the 19th century by the Dutch colonial administration, and after the Second World War, it was continued by the Indonesian government. To a small degree, transmigration occurs even today. It was a program involving the resettling of people from the densely populated areas of mainly Java, but also Bali and Madura, to sparsely populated areas on the islands of Papua, Kalimantan, Sumatra, or Sulawesi. The chief aim of this program was to reduce poverty and overpopulation in Java, which then had about ninety million inhabitants, by offering people jobs in sparsely populated areas where there was a shortage of workforce. Critics nevertheless say that the government in fact used the measure in order to "Javanize" the local population and to undermine possible separatist tendencies in the above-cited localities.

bamboo and wood, and are built with the participation of several villages with whom the departed was in some ways connected (e.g. the place where he or she was born, where he or she lived, where his or her parents or spouse came from, the locality where he or she was active, etc.). It is considered an honour for them to take part in the preparations of such a funeral. If the men of these villages are not invited to participate, they would feel offended – this would indicate they are not regarded as "part of the family". Building material (mainly bamboo and wood) is provided by the family of the deceased, as is food, palm wine and cigarettes for the workmen. After the ceremony, these stands can be dismantled, and the bamboo and wood are used for cooking or building poultry pens, pigsties or buffalo stables.

The guests for whom the stands are made include the extended family (traditional Toraja families had around ten children), friends, and villagers from the localities the departed had links with. Groups bring gifts in the form of buffaloes and pigs, and sometimes also rice and other crops. Eventually, when there is a death in the family of the donor, the roles change – the recipients of the first donation settle their debt. It is expected that the animal given as a gift would have approximately the same value as the one received. Since the period that elapses between two such funerals may stretch for quite a long time, a book is kept where all particulars about the gift are recorded. In the case of donated buffaloes, there is another way of storing information regarding its parameters and quality. After slaughtering the animal, the family of the recipient display its horns on the front of their house. Even many years later both animals can thus be easily compared. Those who are to "repay" the buffalo are aware of this fact and will thus prefer to buy an animal of the same size or even bigger so as not to be spoken ill of.

The *rante* grounds must include *simbuang batu* (stone simbuang). These are stone stelae, of limestone or andesite, either hewn into the form of a block, or left as found in nature (in which case they are mostly cylindrical in shape – see Fig. 2), brought here for the occasion. In many cultures they were seen as sacred objects of worship. In Toraja culture, the *simbuangs* attest to the noble rank of the departed – the more elaborate and longer the ritual, the larger and taller are these stelae.

Another essential attribute of an aristocratic funeral is the *simbuang kayu* (wooden *simbuang*). They are tall trees, uprooted and then brought to the *rante* where they are planted in the earth. After the ceremony they are left where they stand, where in most cases, they gradually wither and die. During the ceremony, buffaloes to be slaughtered are tied to both the *simbuang batu* and *simbuang kayu*, although a majority of these animals are slaughtered in an area between the *tongkonan* (family house) and the granaries.

A wooden tower, *bala'kaan*, is erected near the *simbuangs*, (like the *lakkian* tower, it must not be dismantled), from which cuts of buffalo meat are thrown (see Fig. 17). The custom is called *ma'popendeme'*, and has always been part of funeral rites of the nobility. Nooy-Palm cites that the *tominaa* (priest) would stand on the *bala'kaan* during the act, reciting prayers.[200] Today, two or three men stand on the tower as a rule (they are usually not the *tominaa* anymore), first invoking the names of the ancestors who in the past held important offices or positions (some of these being mythical characters), while throwing meat on the ground. Those who believe themselves to be the descendants of the persons invoked throw themselves at the meat – mostly young boys (see Fig. 18), whose behaviour entertains all present. After this, larger portions of meat are distributed to eminent (living) persons and local authorities. The meat is taken home and only there will it be cooked.

Later, meat is also distributed in the area around the *tongkonan*. This division is called *mantaa*. Depending on social status, all villagers who participate in the organization of the funeral receive an allotted portion. The largest pieces are, to this day, given to the descendants of the nobility, and the smallest to the descendants of slaves. The Catholic Church disapproves of this custom as it reflects social inequality; however, they are aware that it is unrealistic to try to ban it. The Catholic Church therefore resorts to a peculiar tactic, whereby they strive to make the portions of meat for the nobility ever smaller, while the portions meted out to freemen and former slaves ever larger. The Church believes that this measure will eventually lead to a situation where in a few years, everyone will receive roughly equivalent portions of meat.[201] The traditional allocation of meat, however, had its logic. The noblemen received the largest portions, for they were compelled to make a far larger sacrifice, in addition to which they also fed the poor from their sacrificed animals. To this day, the Toraja stress this social aspect of the funerals, claiming that there is no other society where the poor eat as much meat as among the lower orders of the Toraja. The slaughter of a large number of animals was the society's defence mechanism against the accumulation of excessive wealth – in the form of the slaughtered animals, the wealth the aristocracy had acquired would be redistributed during the funeral rites.

Larger funerals have since time immemorial been accompanied by buffalo fights, dancing and chanting, as well as by the *sisemba'* fights, performed according to strict rules. However, today the practice is much more relaxed. As has been said earlier, the buffalo matches could be held only at funerals that

---

200 *Nooy-Palm* 1979, p. 76.
201 Father John Manta', a Catholic priest, May 2006.

lasted more than five days, while the *badong* was danced during rituals lasting no less than three. Today, having cock or buffalo fights is rather problematic, since if these include betting, are classified as gambling, which is illegal in Indonesia.

An inseparable part of the funerals is dancing, the dance most often performed at aristocratic funerals is the *badong*. Male and female dancers stand in a circle facing each other, holding hands and swaying slightly, slowly sidestepping and chanting. The chants deal with an account of the life of the deceased, from birth to death, including the funeral and the pilgrimage of the soul as it departs from the world of humans. Marampa' cites an example of such a song.[202]

> Tu to natampa deata
> Malemo naturu' gaun
> Naempa empa salebu'Sau'ingkokna batara
> Denmo gai'na tangmamma'
> Tang urra'ban bulu mata

> Man who has been created by God
> Now departs with the dew
> He is welcome by the clouds
> Going towards the edge of the firmament
> He leaves behind the fruit of his arduous work
> Why, he was never idle

The *badong* was originally understood as a prayer for the soul of the departed to safely reach the afterworld, and at the same time as a request that the living would continue to be graced with divine blessing. *Tominaa* Toto' Dena' stressed that the *badong* could only be performed after the sacrifice of the first buffalo, at the moment when the departed was now considered ritually dead. He wondered at an incident where the Christians danced the *badong* in the house of someone who had died, but was only to be buried several months hence.[203] Christian church permits the *badong*, but only when the lyrics and purpose of the dance are modified so that it can in no way be connected with *Aluk Todolo*. Kobong cites: "Mourn for the dead, sing funeral songs, dance funeral dances. This is no sin, until you have elevated the dead to a place next to God or above him. Do not put your faith in the souls of dead people as though they could grant a

---

202 *Marampa'* (*Mengenal Toraja*), p. 99. Translated from Indonesian by the author.
203 Several weeks before this conversation, a man told me about this incident. Apparently, people would convene every Wednesday in the house, dancing the *badong*. It is remarkable that although my informant regarded himself as a follower of the *Alukta*, he also took part in these gatherings.

blessing. Blessing and happiness come to us from God's hands alone. But do not use the funeral songs of the infidels. Change the words of the songs, give them a Christian meaning and praise the name of Our Lord."[204]

Another dance to welcome guests is known as the *ma'randing*. In former times this was performed whenever men left for war, and again upon their return. It is danced mostly by two or three older men, but can also involve more participants. They hold shields in their hands, and wear buffalo horns on their heads. The *katia* (see Fig. 11) serves the same purpose. It is danced by women alone, dressed in a traditional costume consisting of a monochromatic skirt and blouse with narrow three-quarter length sleeves, and a characteristic pointed décolletage. They wear tall *sa'pi* hats and the upper section of the body is adorned with *kandaure* ornaments. The *katia* is performed with guests seated along the floor of the stands, smoking the cigarettes they are offered, chewing betel or candy (for more on welcoming the guests, see section 3.3.1).

The funeral rites also include the chanting of mourning songs, accompanied by flute – the *pasauling*. Another musical element is the so-called *musik bambu* (bamboo music). Here, a group of about thirty small boys led by a conductor performs music on wind instruments made of bamboo. This is not indigenous Toraja music, but a cultural import from Northern Sulawesi. Naturally, in older times *musik bambu* did not form part of the funeral rites.

Another feature of funerals (and formerly also of rites celebrating the conclusion of the harvest) is the traditional Toraja sport – *sisemba'*. This is a peculiar type of fighting, where two pairs of young men fight each other.[205] The aim is to knock one's opponents down with kicks as quickly as possible, with the use of the arms being forbidden.[206]

---

204 "Menangisi yang mati, menyanyikan nyanyian ratapan serta menari tarian ratapan itu bukan dosa, asal saja yang mati itu tidak saudara angkat ke samping atau ke atas Tuhan. Janganlah menaruh kepercayaan saudara kepada jiwa orang-orang mati, seakan-akan mereka dapat merestui saudara. Restu dan bahagia, datangnya kepada kita, hanya dari tangan Tuhan saja. Tetapi janganlah saudara memakai nyanyian ratapan orang kafir. Rubahlah kata-kata dari nyanyian balas-balasan, berikanlah makna kekristenan kepadanya, dan pujilah Nama Allah" (*Kobong et al.* 1992, p. 140). Translated from Indonesian by the author. In the original, the author cites that these are so-called *balas-balasan* chants. *Balas-balasan* (Ind.) – to respond to one another. These are chants where participants are divided into two groups, singing in response to one another. These recommendations are listed in a volume titled "Rules of the Adat for Christians", which offer guidance how to be both a good Toraja and a good Protestant (the book was published by the Gereja Toraja – the Toraja Protestant Church).

205 Men forming pairs have their wrists tied to one another (one's right hand is tied to the other's left).

206 *Tominaa* Tato' Dena' told me that formerly *sisemba'* also had the function of a martial art. If an individual was adept at *sisemba'* he could often defeat an adversary armed with a sword. The basic rule to this day remains that if the opponent falls to the ground, it is forbidden to step on him or kick him. Alongside the *sisemba'* there existed another traditional sport, the *sibamba*

Among those dances that are extremely rare today are the *pa'papangan*, performed by young girls to welcome guests. Their graceful movements were accompanied by flute music and the chanting of the mourning song, *pa'marakka*. Another dance – the *ma'dondi* – bears a striking similarity to the *badong*, with even the lyrics being the same – the difference lies in the rhythm. Formerly the *memanna* was only performed at the funeral of a person who had been murdered. The dancers (men only) looked sinister, outfitted in garments made of torn knitted mats and blades of grass tied around their heads. Their weapons were made of bamboo, and their shields from the trunk of the areca palm or the bark of the banana tree. By declaiming horrifying words, the dancers put a curse on the murderer.[207]

3.3 The Actual Catholic Funeral and the Shift in Meaning in Some Rites Practised by Christians

3.3.1 Account of Yohana Maria Sumbung's Funeral

The following section gives an account of an actual funeral – that of Yohana Maria Sumbung, held between May 5–12, 2006, in the vicinity of the *tongkonan* in To' Pao in the Sangalla' region. The deceased was the mother of the Father Stanis, a Catholic priest – one of my main informants, and therefore I had the opportunity to observe not only the entire funeral, but also the several months of preparations which preceded it.

Yohana Maria Sumbung was born on December 1, 1925, in Sangalla' and died on December 19, 2004, in Makassar, from where her body was taken two days later to the house in Kalolu in Tana Toraja, where it was deposited until the beginning of the funeral; that is, for a period of sixteen months. In 1942 she married Felix Dammen (who died in 2002), an eminent local authority who played a major role in promoting education and Catholicism in the Toraja region from as early as the 1940s onwards. Although Yohana Maria Sumbung was from a prominent Catholic family, with one son a Catholic priest and one daughter a nun, due to the fact that the Toraja culture is important to all the Toraja, her funeral was organized a long time after her demise, and it was rather lavish with some elements derived from indigenous ritual.

(performed always after the harvest). This involved men whipping one another with the ribs of palm fronds; however, they were only allowed to lash at the lower section of the body, and it was forbidden to attack the head. The Dutch banned the practice of *sibamba* and the sport perished as a result. According to the *tominaa*, the *sisemba* is likewise illegal today, but is still sometimes performed.

207 *Marampa' (Mengenal Toraja)*, pp. 51 and 100–101.

Description of the Locality in To' Pao

The funeral site in To' Pao was a *tongkonan,* with an entirely new wooden house annexed to the eastern side to provide enough space. Five granaries stood opposite the house, and west of them, the *lakkian* tower, upon which the coffin with the deceased rested for four days. To the east a platform was built for welcoming the guests, and beyond it, many other rostrums to seat them. It was here, in an area enclosed by buildings on all sides, that most of the animals were slaughtered. To the north-east lay the *rante* (open area), where a total of seven *simbuang batu* (stone *simbuangs*) were brought, and *simbuang kayu* (wooden *simbuangs*) such as *ambiri*,[208] *buangin* (*Casuarina equisetifolia*), *kalosi* (*Areca catechu L.* – areca palm) and *induk* (*Arenga saccharifera* – sugar palm). In the vicinity of the *simbuangs* stood the *bala'kaan* (wooden tower), from which the portions of meat were thrown.

Accompanying Activities at the To' Pao Funeral

The *badong* dance was performed in To' Pao during the day, by both professional dancers (men only) clad in black uniforms, who were paid to do so, and by family and guests (both men and women), who danced at night. The evening *badong* was more interesting as well as more emotional, with the men smoking and drinking palm wine as they danced. At one point, the circle split into two parts, where only one half would chant at a time, while the other responded several seconds later. At the head of each procession of the hosts walked a pair of *pasauling* (flute) players, accompanied by a pair of female singers chanting mourning songs. Another musical accompaniment was the *musik bambu* (bamboo music) performed by an ensemble of about thirty young boys. The traditional fight, the *sisemba'*, was rather unusual in To' Pao since it was performed by women, who spontaneously started kicking each other without the formality of forming pairs, to the cries of encouragement and approval on the part of the other guests.

Preparations and Proceedings of the Funeral

Tuesday February 20, 2006
My first visit to the funeral site in To' Pao and the house in Kalolu

In To' Pao, there commenced the construction of a wooden house next to the traditional *tongkonan*. Piled in heaps in front of the *tongkonan* were stalks of

---

208 Father Stanis, a Catholic priest, told me that this is a tree similar to the sugar palm. *Nooy-Palm* (1986, pp. 352 and 360) cites the names such as *ampiri* or *lambiri*, defining the tree as the pseudo-sugar palm.

bamboo several metres long (for the construction of platforms). Otherwise, there were no signs that soon the place would host a funeral with several thousand visitors. I also made my first visit to the house in Kalolu, where the coffin with the deceased was kept.

Thursday March 23, 2006
Purchase of the buffaloes
In the afternoon, Father Stanis, whom I accompanied, purchased five buffaloes at the Bolu market. The animals were later driven in a truck to one of the relative's house and corralled in a nearby bamboo grove.

Friday April 14, 2006
Transferring the deceased from the original coffin to a new one
The day fell on Good Friday. Around seventy people gathered after mass in the house where the coffin with the deceased was deposited. After all were seated on the floor and drank the coffee they were offered (coffee is highly popular with the Toraja, who drink it throughout the day), the gathering was commenced with a prayer led by Father John Manta', a Catholic priest. He then read several passages from the Bible and prayed and sang together with the rest. The general Christian atmosphere was augmented by a small table placed in the centre of the room, with a cross and a pair of candles. About an hour later, the priest went to the next room where the departed was laid out. Here, on the contrary, the atmosphere was distinctly Toraja.[209] About ten old women were crowded around the coffin, sobbing loudly. After a short prayer the priest sprinkled the new coffin with holy water, and the deceased was eventually transferred into it. After dinner, the arrangements for the upcoming funeral were discussed. Old men used bamboo sticks to illustrate what they had in mind. About two hours later, the meeting closed with a final prayer, again recited by Father John. In earlier times, it was customary that before the funeral itself, the closest family convened (the widow or widower, children and the siblings of the deceased, together with the *tominaa*) to discuss issues related to the division of property. Each had to declare how many buffaloes they would provide for the sacrifice. Depending on the number and quality of those, they would then be given a corresponding share of the inheritance. This unique system for the division of inheritance is called *ma'tallang*.

---

209 As stated earlier, all of the walls were covered by red fabric hung with a multitude of adornments.

Monday April 17, 2006
Transferring the coffin from the Kalolu house to the *tongkonan* in To' Pao
Simple provisional shelters were built outside of the house, consisting of a wooden floor (covered with mats) and bamboo pillars, upon which a simple canvas roof was mounted, sheltering the guests from the fierce sun. Meanwhile, around six women were banging bamboo sticks (woody bamboo stalks about 1–1.5 m long) on the *issong*.[210] A mass was served in this area with around two hundred guests in attendance. When the mass was over, the procession with the coffin and several buffaloes set out for To' Pao. Here the coffin was placed in a room in the *tongkonan* decorated in a manner very much similar to the house in Kalolu.

Thursday April 27, 2006
Preparation of the stone stelae – the *simbuang*
Together with Father Stanis I visited a quarry in the Durian Gote area, where about ten men were preparing *simbuangs*. We reached the site when the blocks were already quarried, and the men transferred them onto the truck with the help of a pulley and a bamboo tripod. After several hours of arduous work, the *simbuangs* were brought to To' Pao, where preparations for the funeral were in full swing and most of the platforms to seat the guests were nearly finished. At 8 pm, another gathering accompanied by prayer was held in the *tongkonan*, with about fifty people in attendance. It was similar in character to the gathering of April 14. Again, the arrangements for the funeral were discussed, particularly the number of buffaloes to be sacrificed as well as other affairs related to the upcoming ceremony.

Friday May 5, 2006
First day of the funeral – completion of final preparations
and the sacrifice of the first buffalo
This day was the official start of the funeral. In the afternoon, the first buffalo was slaughtered in front of the *tongkonan*. As mentioned before, in earlier times, it was only from this moment that the deceased was actually regarded as dead. Later the same day, another animal was sacrificed. The men (about two hundred people) who participated in the preparations had been completing the last

---

210 *Issong* (Tor.) – a wooden trough for threshing grains from rice. In Toraja, the activity is referred to as *ma'lambuk*, meaning "knocking out". During a funeral, however, the trough is mostly empty, and only once did I witness it containing rice. The sounds accompanying the threshing are in fact a form of music. Although I have inquired many times regarding the origin and significance of this custom, all I learned was that, at present, it is seen as an expression of respect to all of the assembled guests. Some of my informants told me that in the past, the *ma'lambuk* was mostly performed by female slaves. *Tominaa* Tato' Dena' nonetheless categorically rejected this claim.

arrangements since the morning, some putting finishing touches on the platform set out for the welcome of the guests, others digging holes for the planting of the *simbuangs* or trimming the branches of trees that would be planted in the ground the next day. In front of the house, several women were performing the *ma'lambuk* (threshing); around fourteen buffaloes were present here and in the adjoining *rante* in order to lend the ceremony the requisite pomp. At one point, a fight erupted abruptly among some of these animals, wreaking a bit of havoc. At 5 pm, the so-called opening prayer took place on this site.

Saturday May 6, 2006
Second day of the funeral – transferring the dead from the *tongkonan* to the granary

Early in the morning, the stone *simbuangs* were erected on a slope (see Fig. 13) as were the trees, *ambiri, buangin, kalosi,* and *induk.* The central figure of this ritual was Father John, clad in an alb and stole, with a Toraja dagger at his waist and a Bible in his hands (see Fig. 12). First he said a prayer at the *simbuangs* sprinkling them with holy water, and then he repeated the same proceedings with the buffaloes. One would be hard pressed to find an image that would more visibly epitomize the coexistence of autochthonous Toraja culture with its newly-adopted Christianity. This rite over, some men took part in finishing the wooden tower – the *bala'kaan* – at the bottom of which a buffalo was sacrificed in the afternoon (two buffaloes were slaughtered on this day).[211] Another important step was the transferring of the coffin from the *tongkonan* to the granary. In the room where she lay at rest gathered mainly the grandchildren and siblings of the departed. After prayer, many of them approached the feet of the dead woman, embracing them and thus bidding farewell to her. They knew that the coffin would soon be sealed and that they would see the deceased for the last time. Before carrying the coffin from the *tongkonan,* some danced the *badong* in the house, others dressed the *tau-tau* statue, or tied the *lamba-lamba,* a several metre-long red fabric, to the coffin. The women again performed the *ma'lambuk* outside the house; on this day, however, they were actually threshing the rice, although the quantity of grain was merely symbolic. The men first lifted the coffin, starting to move and shake it. According to *Aluk Todolo,* the custom was practised in order to make the soul confused and displeased with this world, and to wish to depart from it as soon as possible. After this they issued out of the house with the coffin and the *tau-tau* statue to the granary, where the coffin was deposited until Monday. During the day, several communal prayers took place under the guardianship of Father John.

---

211 Pigs were slaughtered throughout the entire funeral. In total, they amounted to hundreds.

Sunday May 7, 2006
Holiday
Apart from the prayer for closest family at 7 pm, there were no other ceremonies. All Toraja Catholics observe Sunday as a holiday and it is thus not counted among the days of the funeral.

Monday May 8, 2006
Third day of the funeral – procession through the village, transferring the deceased to the *lakkian* (tower)
From the early morning, the men were busy making *belo tedong* (lit. buffalo adornment) and *parangka* (lit. branch). *Belo tedong* is a triangular adornment made of red fabric with a grey hem, with daggers and gold bracelets fastened in the centre (in To' Pao, there was one dagger and a pair of bracelets). From the sides protruded stalks of young bamboo about one metre long, as well as other plants with various bits of old fabric tied to them; tradition has it that these are endowed with magical power. The men carry the *belo tedong* before the buffaloes in a procession through the village. The *parangka* is a decoration several metres tall. Its framework is made of strong bamboo and covered in red cloth with smaller bamboo stalks with strips of ancient fabrics fastened to them on both sides at an angle of about forty degrees. The *parangku* is likewise carried through the village in a procession, and subsequently displayed in front of the *lakkian* tower. Meanwhile, other men have prepared the *pradula* – the sarcophagus; a rectangular wooden pedestal upon which the coffin is placed and covered with a lid in the form of the roof of the traditional house, *tongkonan*. The men attach a bamboo construction underneath the *pradula* sarcophagus in order to be better able to carry it. Outside the house, the *pa'piong,* a repast made of five pigs slaughtered early that morning, was being cooked in bamboo over a fire. Four women performed a symbolic threshing of rice in front of the house, while females clad in red danced the *katia*, after which the coffin was moved from the granary to the sarcophagus. Professional dancers together with the family performed the *badong*, Father John delivered a prayer, and just after noon,[212] the procession of several hundred participants set out on a journey around the village – this part of the ritual is called *ma'pasonglo'* (lit. to go down). At the helm walked men leading almost thirty buffaloes with their horns adorned with red cloth, and the procession featured *belo tedong* and *parangka* decorations. The men were followed by seven children clad in traditional attire, one of them carrying a photograph of the departed. The family walked behind them under

---

212 The custom according to which the rites connected with death had to be performed only after noon is derived from *Aluk Todolo*. Christians today nonetheless admit this only grudgingly.

the red fabric – *lamba-lamba* – mostly in pairs (see Fig. 20); the procession finished with men carrying the sarcophagus and the *tau-tau* statue reminiscent of the deceased.[213] On their way, they jumped around, making various movements with the coffin, even turning in circles with it at the crossroads. After going full circle in a rather taxing terrain and climate,[214] everyone returned to To' Pao. The coffin was brought to the *lakkian*, (wooden tower) where it would rest until the last day of the funeral – Friday. In the afternoon, several buffaloes were slaughtered in the *rante* area. Later, the welcoming of the guests began. Groups of about a hundred people each arrived at the platform built for this purpose, bringing with them buffaloes and pigs.[215] The animals were then temporarily placed in an area in front of the platform. Formerly the guests would be solemnly announced by the loud recital of their entire family tree, but today they are usually welcomed with several claps of the gong. Before entering the platform, members of each group separated according to gender and seated themselves on the floor in places assigned to them. They were subsequently followed by family members led by the *to ma'doloan* (lit. the man walking in front),[216] a pair of flautists and two female singers of mourning chants who arrived to welcome them. The women acting as hosts offered the female part of the congregation betel from a gold casket known as the *pa'panganan* or from small black pouches – the *sepu'*. Chewing betel is no longer as widespread in Indonesia as it has been in the past, and when there are mothers with children present among the guests, often only candy is served, as was the case with this funeral. With men, this part of the ceremony was similar except that they were offered cigarettes. In the meantime, female dancers performed the *ka'tia* in front of the platform to provide entertainment for the guests. The hosts would then retire, and dozens of women appeared on the stage, offering the guests coffee and cakes. The women dancing the *ka'tia* were replaced by male dancers performing the *badong*. About fifteen minutes later, the women offering refreshments left, and then the guests followed them to the accompaniment of

---

213 The *lamba-lamba* cloth forms a pair with the *parangka* adornment. The *parangka* symbolizes the vertical connection of man and God, and the *lamba-lamba* represents the horizontal connection of all humankind – the women and children walking under the cloth at the helm of the procession, the departed carried by the men, and the men walking at the end of the procession. Father Stanis, May 2006.

214 Although part of the route was through the village on an asphalt road, another was through a narrow forest path. The worst hardship was the unbearable heat; women frequently distributed cups of water during the procession.

215 Upon arriving to the funeral site, guests entered the animals they brought into a register and paid the mandatory tax. A separate shelter was erected for them, where several officials in charge of collecting taxes in the region were at work.

216 Formerly this function was performed by slaves connected to the family of the deceased. At present, the *to ma'doloan* are paid for this work.

musik bambu performed by a thirty-strong orchestra of children playing wind instruments; the guests then scattered to their assigned places on the platforms. These platforms were divided into several sections, each assigned to one of the children of the deceased.[217] The welcoming ceremony would then immediately repeat itself with the next group of guests. The itinerary included buffalo fights, which took place late in the afternoon. The day closed with communal prayers interspersed with orations by various family members and later also performances of a number of choirs.

Tuesday May 9, 2006
Fourth day of the funeral – the welcoming of guests
Everything that took place over the course of the day was part of the ceremony of welcoming guests according to the rules described above. Three buffaloes were sacrificed, and in the afternoon, meat was divided from the *bala'kaan* tower.

Wednesday May 10, 2006
Fifth day of the funeral – the welcoming of guests
The Wednesday itinerary was identical with that of Tuesday; four buffaloes were slaughtered. Men (and also several women) danced the *badong* from the evening until four in the morning, drinking palm wine (mostly from glasses, but sometimes also from bamboo) and having fun.

Thursday May 11, 2006
Sixth day of the funeral – the sacrifice of the remaining animals
Outside of the house and in the *rante* area by the *simbuangs,* all the remaining buffaloes were slaughtered (see Figs. 14 and 15), this amounted to about thirty animals. All the remaining pigs were slaughtered too. Afterwards, the meat was divided among the guests.

Friday May 12, 2006
Seventh day of the funeral – mass in the church and burying the deceased in a tomb
The coffin was carried down from the *lakkian* (wooden tower) and placed on a sarcophagus, the *pradula* (which had already been used on Monday in the procession through the village), where the relatives – in all about two hundred people – took photographs for a long time. After that, they danced the *badong* for the last time; again, some women beat bamboo sticks against a wooden

---

217 Kitchens were attached to each of the platforms, providing victuals for the funeral guests several times daily. The meals were usually made of the sacrificed animals and were served with vegetables and rice.

trough, the *issong* and all guests prayed before leaving To' Pao. The procession which also featured the statue *tau-tau* first headed to the church, where a two-hour long requiem mass was served, officiated by the bishop and several priests, including the son of the deceased – Father Stanis. From the church, the sarcophagus was then carried to the tomb, the *patane*, where the husband of the deceased – Felix Dammen – was already interred. After sealing the tomb, the bereaved went to the house in Kalolu, where a final communal dinner was served. Afterwards the family with the bishop took photographs outside of the house.

The funeral of Yohana Maria Sumbung that took place in To' Pao in May 2006 lasted altogether eight days, and was attended by thousands of guests (the son of the deceased, Father Stanis, believes that there were up to ten thousand people). Around thirty buffaloes and hundreds of pigs were sacrificed.

3.3.2 The Shift in Meaning in Some Rites Practised by Christians

As it transpires in some of the examples mentioned throughout the work, Christians have largely preserved many original indigenous customs and continue to practise them. Often, however, there has occurred a seminal shift in their meaning, and thus the reason why such rites are performed today has also changed accordingly. This section of my work presents insights and findings I gathered in this regard, mostly on the basis of several conversations held with the Father John in May 2006.

As has already been stated, according to *Aluk Todolo,* the souls of sacrificed animals were to assist the soul of the departed on its journey to the realm of *puya*. Christians claim today that the animals are slaughtered solely to provide repast for the guests. I believe this is only partly true. The slaughter of buffaloes and pigs during a funeral rite is in fact so deeply rooted in the Toraja identity that it cannot be renounced, even after the adoption of Christianity.

In former times, the man slaughtering the buffalo first had to strike the machete into the soil and recite a prayer asking the deity of the given area for permission to slaughter the animal on that site. Today, Christians pray to God to forgive them the killing of a living creature.

In the past, the Toraja collected the buffalo blood[218] which gushed from the throat of the animal as it was struck with the machete in a vessel made of

---

218 It was believed that blood has regenerative effects. During an *Alukta* ceremony held on the occasion of repairing a house, I saw one man daubing his thigh with blood in order to ensure good health. In the past, older fabrics were likewise smeared with blood so as not to lose their magical powers.

bamboo. A small portion of this would then be cooked and used as one of the ingredients necessary for preparing the sacrificial *pesung*. Blood was also used to improve the taste of a dish named *pa'piong*, consisting of meat, vegetables and spices, a practice which has continued to this day (except in the case of the Pentecostalists – see section 3.4.4).

In the past, it was customary to publicly announce the number and type of buffaloes sacrificed by the descendants of the deceased. Christians disapprove of this custom, just as they disapprove of dividing the property of the departed on the basis of the number of slaughtered animals. They regard the custom as unjust, and yet ever so often continue to practise it; their attitude to the distribution of the meat is similar.

According to the rules of *Aluk Todolo*, when mounting the *simbuang*, people prayed to the deity of the given place to permit them to erect a stone or a tree in the given area. Christians today address their God during this rite, praying for success of the ritual.

The men jumping with the coffin today represent merely a custom without any deeper meaning. A similar approach is taken to the ancient cloths which are displayed on the day of the funeral, and attached to the *belo tedong* and *parangka* adornments for the procession day. According to *Aluk Todolo,* these artefacts had a magical power, but today their function is reduced to that of a decorative accessory.

At the time when society was still strictly stratified, certain activities were assigned to the slaves – for example carrying pigs to the funeral site. Today, nobody wants to undertake this task, and thus typically young boys are assigned to carry the pigs, or somebody is hired to do so. In some instances, such as with help in the kitchen, the problem is solved by employing others who will perform these duties.

It might appear at first glance that there are no major differences between Christian and *Aluk Todolo* funeral rites. On closer scrutiny it becomes evident that the function and symbolism of the latter has been considerably modified so as to be in keeping with Christian principles and requirements. The cited changes aptly illustrate the visible shift in the traditional understanding of rituals.

3.4   Toraja Pentecostalists and Their Funerals

The followers of the Pentecostal Movement[219] in the Toraja region differ in their view on the form of funeral rites from most members of other Christian denominations in the region. It is precisely the extremity of their position that made me keen to take a closer look. The Pentecostalists regard the Bible as an absolute authority, and it is in fact their literal interpretation of it that distinguishes them from other Christians. This literal reading lies at the root of their total disapproval of incorporating many features originating from the *Aluk Todolo* into present-day Toraja Christian funeral rites. Other Torajas are often derisive about devotees of the Pentecostalist movement, demurring that they sing too often, clapping their hands as they do,[220] and noting they have a ban on eating blood and slaughtering buffaloes and pigs at funerals. Often they disparagingly observe that the adherents of Pentecostalism only converted to the movement in order to extricate themselves from the unending and extremely financially taxing cycle of donating and receiving animals during funerals.

3.4.1 The Funeral of Ne' Tappi and Interview with Her Son, Duma' Rante Tasik

On February 12–13, 2006, I was present at the funeral of the ninety-five year old Ne' Tappi in the village of Tonga, where I met my informants: the son of the deceased, Mr. Duma' Rante Tasik, the Pastor Nehemia Tangkin, who officiated the mass during this rite, and his wife, Saarah Salino, who likewise performed the functions of a preacher.

Even at first glance, this Pentecostalist funeral differed from other Protestant or Catholic rites. During his sermon as well as the mass, the pastor, delivered his service very emotionally; his wife, who alternated with him several times during the prayers, behaved in a similar manner. Apart from the exalted verbal addresses, the ritual also differed in other aspects – inseparably including as it did the frequent singing of hymns, which were rather untraditionally accompanied by guitar playing. The rostrums were not decorated with red cloth

---

219 Derived from *pentecoste* (Gk.) meaning the fiftieth – the Fiftieth day after Easter Sunday; the Pentecost celebrates the descent of the Holy Spirit upon Earth. The movement emerged in the United States at the beginning of the 20th century and adheres to the Protestant Church. In Tana Toraja and Toraja Utara there are in total 13 denominations of Pentecostalism.

220 The Pentecostalist rites are indeed notorious for including more songs than other Christian denominations. On the whole, their songs are also more spirited and faster (with the exception of funeral hymns), and are often accompanied by musical instruments, such as the guitar, drums, or the organ.

featuring Toraja motifs, and children in traditional costumes were also absent. On the other hand, as is with other funerals, bamboo platforms were erected in the immediate vicinity of the house and in its close surroundings. Similar to other rites, upon arrival, guests were welcomed with betel, cigarettes and sweets, and were offered a repast of buffalo and pig meat. The two-day long funeral ceremony featured neither dancing nor other activities (the sole program was comprised of prayers and choral singing accompanied by guitar) and concluded with the burial of the deceased in a crevice in a rock created by erosion.

During my conversation with the son of the deceased – Mr. Duma' Rante Tasik,[221] in March 2006, I tried to find out why the adherents of this movement are not allowed to slaughter buffaloes or pigs at their funerals. In the end it transpired that the respondent would not be able to provide me with this information. He himself had abandoned the custom at the bidding of the pastor, whom he did not want to anger or disappoint.

However, based on his claims I then mistakenly assumed that Pentecostalists probably have some sort of a taboo regarding the slaughter of buffaloes and pigs on the site where the funeral ceremony is held. Only later did I find (from Nehemia Tangkin and his wife Saarah Salino) that animals must not be slaughtered at all (no matter where) due to the fact that it is obviously a habit adopted from the original religion *Aluk Todolo*. Therefore, it is not acceptable for the Pentecostal pastors to continue practising such a ritual. Toraja followers of Pentecostalism often find themselves in a tricky predicament during funerals – on the one hand, there is the disapproval from the Church, which explicitly bans the sacrifice of animals, and on the other, pressure from family members of different confessions, to whom a funeral without buffaloes and pigs is not a real funeral. My respondent found himself in this unpleasant situation, as his family forced him to sacrifice at least one buffalo and several pigs far from the house. He confided this to me in a quiet voice, as if apologising for the breaking of prescripts set by the Pentecostal Movement. If a buffalo is slaughtered at the funeral site, the pastors as well as other Pentecostalist adherents refuse to partake of the offered repast during the ceremony, which causes other complications.[222]

---

221 Mr. Duma' Rante Tasik was born in 1941 into a Protestant family; in 1967 he nonetheless became an adherent of the Pentecostal Movement. His deceased mother had converted to Pentecostalism at the age of 85, that is, ten years prior to her death, for purely pragmatic reasons. At that time she was no longer able to attend her Protestant congregation, which lay too far from her home. Unlike the respondent and his daughter, I found this to be a rather peculiar reason for religious conversion.

222 Some Pentecostalist ministers indeed refuse to eat the offered repast in protest against the sacrifice of animals, sometimes going as far as to refuse to serve mass. Such a predicament nonetheless happens only sporadically, since the members of the congregation are well aware that with a high-principled minister, they cannot afford to break the ban.

3.4.2 Information Provided by Pastor Nehemia Tangkin and His Wife Saarah Salino

The essential information explaining why the sacrifice of animals at Pentecostal funerals is forbidden was eventually gleaned from an interview with Pastor Nehemia Tangkin and his wife in April 2006. In addition, the informants spoke about the issues regarding the rejection of other elements originating from the *Alukta*, and later, expanded on other differences which were, nevertheless, unrelated to the original religion, instead deriving from the specificities of Pentecostalism.

It transpired from the interview that Pentecostalists do not use decorations during the funerals, but on the other hand, neither do they explicitly ban them. This is also true of other customs (e.g. the welcoming of guests or dances) that are commonly observed at other Toraja Christian funerals. Pentecostalists thus positively do not sanction any rites that are in direct contradiction of the Bible, and also try to limit the practice of the remaining customs. They try to make at least that part of the funeral which takes place in the public resemble as much as possible the Christian funeral rites of other ethnic groups, and to contain the fewest possible elements of Toraja culture.

According to Saraah Salino, the manner in which the Toraja dispense their finances is unethical. Often when someone falls ill, the family is unable to provide the funds necessary to pay a visit to the doctor or receive treatment in a hospital. Yet as soon as the patient actually dies, the family suddenly has enough money to hold a costly funeral; everyone shows respect to the deceased posthumously, with hundreds of people attending the funeral. She went as far as to say that many Toraja live in poverty throughout their life, so destitute even as to be unable to afford fish or other meat, often subsisting on rice alone. Yet once there is a death in the family, finances necessary for the purchase of buffaloes must be found at all costs.

The pastor Nehemia Tangkin, who at first struck me as a most ardent Pentecostalist, would later observe that most adherents of the Pentecostal movement are too extreme in their interpretation of the Bible, while he considers himself to be one of the liberal pastors. In particular, he pointed out the problems related to the partaking of the meat of buffaloes and pigs sacrificed at funerals. Some Pentecostalist pastors refuse to partake of this meat for several reasons. In the case of *Alukta* funerals, where the animals are sacrificed to the deceased, or to his soul, it is unthinkable for most pastors to eat their flesh. With some denominations of the Pentecostal movement, sacrifice is forbidden altogether, and fish and chicken are used as an alternative solution for feeding the guests, which had not traditionally been served at *Alukta* funeral rites. With other denominations, animal sacrifices are only allowed according to a strict set of rules – when a pastor consents to the killing of a set number of animals for the purposes of immediate consumption, he would naturally also eat together with the funeral guests. Some pastors of the Pentecostal movement, though, refuse to eat meat even at the funerals of other Protestants or members of other Christian denominations. Mr. Nehemia partly condemned this behaviour, saying that food should never become a cause of strife among people. He supported his argument with an analogy to the dictum of Apostle Paul – that being among the pagans does not also make one a pagan. Mr. Nehemia thus accepts the food so as not to offend his host, but never takes any raw meat back home with him.[223] On the other hand, however, he is aware of the fact that food should never impose sin on a friend, a prescript allegedly present even in the Bible,[224] and thus fears that if his co-religionists saw him partaking of meat, this could cause them embarrassment. Thus, if other Pentecostalists are present at the funeral, he would not partake of the meat of either buffaloes or pigs, instead restricting himself to fish or chicken, setting an example to others. Given the existence of no less than 13 denominations of Pentecostalism in Tana Toraja and the absence of any centralization, the views and principles of individual pastors may differ in part, something that is not as usual with other churches.

3.4.3 Interview with Pastor Yunus Padang

On Nehemia Tangkin's recommendation I later met the experienced and successful pastor Yunus Padang.[225] Compared to Nehemia Tangkin, he made a more vigorous impression; his views were uncompromising and throughout, he consistently and sharply criticised the attitude of Toraja of other Christian denominations towards the form of contemporary funeral rites. In particular, he was against the fact that even today the dead exercise a crucial influence on the functioning of society, and that the tenets of *Aluk Todolo* continue to have a major impact on the life of the Toraja of Christian persuasion.

---

223 This would already be binding, for he would have to return the meat in the future, thus implicating himself into the cycle of giving and taking that the Pentecostalists are actively against.
224 I believe he had in mind the First Epistle to the Corinthians, 8, 4–13.
225 The number of registered members of the religion is important to Pentecostalist pastors, since they do not receive any payment from the Church, rather their churchmen pay them 10 % of their income every month. According to public opinion, a successful pastor of the Pentecostal Movement can get up to 4,000 US dollars per month.

Interview no. 7

Y. P.:[226] Animal sacrifice is just so much of a waste. At the moment, one buffalo
costs more than one hundred million,[227] about one hundred and ten to one
hundred and twenty in fact![228] A single buffalo! So it is not just for food.
This is true of Protestants, Toraja Catholics, and even some denominations
of Pentecostalism, who continue to sacrifice in this manner. But as for the
Church itself, who would be willing to donate to it one hundred million?

M. B.: Yes.

Y. P.: The buffalo is God's gift, God created it, God gave it breath (*life*), it is
thanks to God that the grass grows, and yet we make sacrifices to the dead.
And it is not for the sake of food alone. If it were just for food, they could
easily buy an unsightly one. Yes, a buffalo or a female that is no longer fertile,
but the locals won't have it, they won't slaughter such animals. If the animal
is (*seen as*) defective, such as having damaged horns or a broken tail, they
won't sacrifice it. So you can be sure that there is a connection to the dead.
I wrote in my Bachelor thesis that the dead continue to exercise so strong
an influence over the living, that the latter are willing to spend all of their
fortune on the dead. When there no longer exists a connection to the spirits
of the ancestors, it will no longer matter, this will not be a problem. Like in
Manado,[229] in Java, in Jakarta, when there is a funeral, a pig is slaughtered,
a cow is slaughtered, there is no taboo, there is no connection with the
deceased (*the animal is killed*) really for food alone. But here it is not for food,
and there is proof for that. You can tell from the value of the buffalo or the
pig. For neither can you bring just any pig, it must not be a female, it must
be a male. Why, would a dead man refuse a female? The meat of the female
tastes the same as that of the male. But why does this distinction have to be
made? It derives from the indigenous religion.

It transpires from my interviews that of all the Christian denominations,
the Pentecostalists are the least tolerant to the presence of *Alukta* elements in
funeral rituals. The intensity of this refusal of Toraja elements differs depending
on the respective denominations, but also on the attitude of each individual
pastor, a phenomenon made possible due to the great degree of autonomy of
the Pentecostal movement.

---

226 Yunus Padang.
227 The respondent here has in mind the *tedong saleko*.
228 The equivalent of 10,000–12,000 US dollars.
229 City in the north of Sulawesi.

3.4.4 Practices Rejected by Pentecostalists

The following list presents the practices that are rejected by Pentecostalists. I also furnish the rationale behind their stance, as well as the original purpose of each of these practices.

The Slaughtering of Buffaloes and Pigs During Funeral Rites
According to Pastor Nehemia Tangkin, the Pentecostalists see in the slaughter of animals a clear connection to the original local religion, which as followers of another confession – Christianity – they cannot accept. Some Protestants and Catholics counter this by claiming that though they have long abandoned the *Alukta*, they continue to sacrifice animals in order to honour the ancestral traditions of previous generations. This claim is nonetheless unacceptable for the more uncompromising Pentecostalists. The price of animals is so exorbitant that many families run into debt for decades to come. Pentecostalists claim that if someone is forced to borrow money, this means that he or she are in a dire economic predicament and it is thus wrong to exacerbate it even further. Aside from this, Pentecostalists regard the slaughter of costly animals as an ill-advised waste of money[230] that could be more meaningfully invested in some long-term beneficial purpose. The pastor cited as an example the social sphere – the schooling or development of public spaces and infrastructure. Some denominations sanction the sacrifice of buffaloes and pigs only on the condition that their meat is used immediately on the spot for preparing a repast for funeral guests, and not allotted to individual persons in a raw condition, as is otherwise common practice. This nevertheless involves a number of problems, as it is very difficult to establish the exact number of buffaloes necessary for feeding the guests at a given funeral.

The Consumption of Meat from Sacrificed Animals at *Alukta* Funerals
Originally, animals were sacrificed to the deceased, or to their souls, after which the guests ate the meat. Pentecostalists forbid the partaking of meat that has a relationship to the deceased and his or her soul. They derive this taboo from the Bible.[231]

The Partaking of Buffalo Blood
As I have discussed earlier, Christians commonly use blood to improve the taste of certain dishes. Pentecostalists, however, are vehemently opposed to the

---

230 The prices of buffaloes are cited earlier in the present work (see section 2.4.5). A pig cost between 80–100 US dollars in 2006.
231 Psalms 106, 28–29.

partaking of blood, claiming that it is in the blood that the animals' souls reside. They derive this claim from the Bible, specifically from the Book of Genesis and the Acts of the Apostles.[232]

Traditional System of Dividing Inheritance

The adherents of the Pentecostalist movement are opposed to the system of dividing inheritance based on the number of buffaloes sacrificed by each member of the family; they regard this as unjust and in contradiction to the Bible. According to them, people should love one another and help one another in distress, and in particular the stronger should help the weak. They believe that the absurd "competition" they see as part of the funeral rites effectively denies all spiritual values represented by Christianity. They also argue that the drawback of this sort of division is the exacerbation of financial differences between the members of the family, whereby the poor become even more impoverished as the rich get richer. Another major problem is the fact that children without means who wish to come into at least a part of the fortune of their parents frequently run into debt in order to purchase the buffaloes to guarantee them their inheritance. Later, they are unable to repay the exorbitant sums borrowed, and thus paradoxically, the inheritance in the end often falls to the creditor. Pentecostalists also criticise the fact that many Toraja die in debt, as according to their belief, these people end up in hell after they die. Large debts are then shifted onto the next generation, for few people are able to cope with such an enormous financial burden.

Funerals Held with a Distance of Several Months or Years from Death

As cited above, even to this day, Toraja funerals of both the adherents of *Aluk Todolo* and Christians take place over a period ranging from several months to several years after death. Pastors of the Pentecostal movement, however, try to see that members of their congregation are buried within eight days from their demise at the latest. They believe that this period is sufficient to allow for tidings to travel to all friends and relatives, and to enable the family to prepare the funeral. By hastening the funeral, they wish to prevent the relatives of other religious persuasion from purchasing buffaloes. Another reason why the Pentecostalists are trying to expedite the funeral ritual is the fact that according to the rules of the *Alukta,* certain restrictions come into effect within the community up until the point

---

232 Genesis 9: 3–4. In the King James translation: *Every moving thing that liveth shall be meat for you; even as the green herb have I given you all things. But flesh with the life thereof, which is the blood thereof, shall ye not eat.* The word "soul" does not occur. In the Indonesian version, however, it actually occurs in the fourth verse: *Hanya daging yang masih ada nyawanya, yakni darahnya, janganlah kamu makan.* (You shall not eat only the meat that still has soul.) Acts 15:20 and Acts 15:29.

when the deceased is buried. These regarded the performance of the rituals of life *rambu tuka'* (smoke ascending rituals) – thus during this period the inhabitants of the given locality could not be married, could not celebrate the arrival of a baby, or perform the rite celebrating the erection or repairs of the *tongkonan*, the traditional house. To this day, villagers partly observe these tenets. The adherents of the Pentecostalist movement take objection both to the fact that these norms originate in the *Alukta*, and that the "dead dictate the running of society".

Allotment of the Meat

Apart from objecting to the slaughtering of buffaloes, Pentecostalists regard the allocation of the meat as undemocratic, for it is based on social stratification, which contradicts the Bible and Christian principles.

Pentecostalists condemn the sacrifice of buffaloes and pigs during funeral rites, for they perceive in it a connection to the ancestral faith. Some pastors of the Pentecostal movement do not accept the argument of other Christians that animals are slaughtered today chiefly in order to serve as repast for funeral guests. This opinion derives – among other things – from the price of buffalo, which exceeds the actual value of the animal manifold. The pastors likewise point out the negative effects of the sacrifice: the expenditure of money and resultant debt, which frequently accompany funerals in contravention to the Bible. Pentecostalists also actively oppose practices related to the sense of belonging to a certain social class. Thus for instance, they oppose the non-democratic allotment of raw meat, and the division of inheritance based on the number of buffaloes sacrificed by the children of the deceased. As mentioned earlier, the Pentecostalists require that the deceased be buried within eight days after death at the latest. This measure is designed to prevent holding large funerals with a large number of sacrificed animals.

3.5 Toraja Muslims

Muslims form roughly 7% of the total population of Tana Toraja and Toraja Utara; as a rule, these are foreigners and their Toraja spouses who have converted to Islam, as well as their progeny who are mostly Muslim. Islamic law which bans the consumption of pork and alcohol also decrees that the deceased be buried within twenty-four hours from demise. Islam is thus in considerable contradiction with Toraja culture, an integral part of which are funerals held over many weeks, months, or even years after death, and accompanied by the consumption of pork and palm wine. Muslims who wish to reconcile Islam with Toraja culture solve this conundrum by holding subsequent rites which include the sacrifice of buffaloes.

3.5.1 Toraja Muslim Death-Related Rites

Like all Muslims, their religion prescribes that the Toraja Muslims have but four duties with respect to funerals: the dead must be washed, wrapped in white fabric, they must be prayed for, and they must be buried at the latest within twenty-four hours after death. Ideally, the body should be washed three times, but if conditions do not allow for this, one washing is considered sufficient. Men are wrapped in one to three layers of cloth, women in three to five. The body is tied with string in five places – in the areas of the head, chest, waist, knees and ankles. After it is deposited in the grave, the knots are untied which symbolically enables the deceased to become one with the earth. His or her head must point to the north, and the feet to the south, while the body is turned slightly to the west, so that the face can be directed towards Mecca.

The Muslim Toraja perform several other rites following the funeral. There may be up to seven in total, their number and character nonetheless differ depending on the wishes and financial standing of the family of the deceased. These rites are named after the number of days that have elapsed since the funeral. *Malam pertama* (the first night) follows immediately after the funeral; members of the family and neighbours gather at that time, mostly in the house where the deceased lived. They pray for the deceased and console the bereaved, as the imam delivers a sermon on the Muslim perspective on life and death. All that is served is coffee, tea and cakes. *Malam kedua* (the second night) is identical to the first night. During the *malam ketiga* (third night) the family of the deceased likewise devote themselves to prayer, passages from the Qur'an are read, but this time dinner is also served. Depending on the financial capability of the family, a buffalo, a goat, or chickens may be sacrificed. *Malam ketujuh* (seventh night) is very much the same as the third night. Some families also celebrate the *malam sembilan* (the ninth night); the most significant, however, is the *malam empat puluh* (fortieth night) which I will discuss in greater detail in section 3.5.2. *Malam seratus* (the hundredth night) is not held as frequently as the ritual connected with the fortieth night, its nature, however, is very similar, differing only in that there are fewer guests at the hundredth night. Again, the event consists mainly of prayers, as family members, friends and neighbours congregate, and buffaloes are slaughtered.

Between April 1–2, 2006 I had the opportunity to be present at a Muslim funeral rite *malam empat puluh* in Rantepao, held by Mrs. Nurhayati – daughter of the deceased, Mr. Satu (1921–2006). I gained all information relating to Toraja Muslim death-related rituals during this rite – observing the proceedings and speaking to the participants. Later I visited the office of the Ministry of Religion in Makale, where I was given a book on Islam; after studying this,

I visited the office again and consulted all that was unclear with Mr. Arifuddin. Further information was supplied by Mr. Bumbun Pakata, who acted as the religious leader reading the prayers from the Qur'an at the ritual on April 1. He is a recognized Muslim authority in Rantepao; some years previously he had in fact undertaken the pilgrimage to Mecca. With Mrs. Nurhayati, I discussed the fortieth night and the preparations related to it.

3.5.2 *Malam Empat Puluh* (The Fortieth Night)

Family members gather as a rule several days before the celebration of the fortieth night – *malam empat puluh* in order to discuss the logistics of the upcoming ritual, and agree on the number of buffaloes to be slaughtered. The deceased, Mr. Satu, no longer had any siblings, thus the group present at the meeting, apart from his wife, included only three of his children, since the others either did not wish to or could not be present. The family then waited for the buffaloes and pigs to become available on market day (held every six days in the nearby town of Bolu), where they purchased the buffaloes and other necessary items.

The Toraja Muslims believe that after forty days have elapsed since the demise, the soul of the deceased finally takes leave of his or her house. Mr. Bumbun Pakata stressed several times, that this ritual bears no relation to Islam, instead forming part of tradition. He was unable to specify this statement, nevertheless he claimed that it was not by any means a Toraja tradition. Since Islam came to the Toraja region from surrounding areas inhabited by the Bugis Muslims, the origin of the custom most likely lies in their culture.

After evening prayers on the fortieth night, guests started to convene in the house of the deceased – family members and neighbours as well as friends of various faiths. The members of the family prepared various favourite items to furnish the soul of the deceased for its journey, rolling them up in a mattress that had belonged to the deceased.[233] These included some clothes, a plate and other everyday articles. This bundle would be carried early the next morning to the person (family member or friend) who had been entrusted to read the prayers the night before. This gift may nevertheless go to another person – the poor, as a rule. The rest of the clothes of the deceased are then given out to Muslim friends. Mrs. Nurhayati did not know where this custom came from; it is practised by many Toraja Muslims, but she was aware that

---

233 Mrs. Nurhayati bought a new mattress as she would be ashamed to display the old one before the others.

it did not originate in Islam and neither does it form part of Toraja culture. Formally dressed guests of honour sat in several rows on the floor of the house throughout the evening, reading prayers from the Qur'an. The decoration of the room featured no Toraja attributes (the walls were not covered in red cloth, nor were there daggers, *kandaure* bead decorations, or swords), still, it was decorated for the ceremony in another manner – the air was fragrant with joss sticks, while pyramids of sticky rice, bananas and other fruit were piled on plates. Other guests sat outside the house, where temporary bamboo platforms were erected – these were decorated in the same manner as at other Toraja funerals, with red cloth featuring Toraja motifs. After supper, the guests would slowly disperse.

Before six o'clock the following morning, two buffaloes were slaughtered on the grounds behind the house; a morning sacrifice would be out of the question with an *Alukta* funeral under any circumstances, as animals can only be sacrificed after twelve o'clock. At Muslim funerals, buffaloes can be slaughtered only by a man who meets two basic criteria. Firstly, he must be Muslim – should the buffalo be slaughtered by a person of another confession, or should a prayer be omitted before slaughter, Muslims would refuse to partake of such meat. Secondly, he must be able to slaughter the animal according to Islamic law, applied by all Muslims in slaughtering all animals. The buffalo is first tied up, with its mouth turned to the west and its whole head pointing to the south, the feet to the north; the person performing the slaughter must pronounce *Bismillahi Allahu Akbar* (In the Name of God, God is Great). Unlike Christians, the Muslims do not regard the slaughter of a buffalo as a heroic act – first of all they tie the animal up in order to secure it in the necessary position; thus human cunning (several men using various ropes with nooses) within seconds transforms the majestic creature into a helpless victim. To cut the throat of a buffalo thus immobilized is an easy matter – the animal bleeds to death almost immediately, and its death is very fast. The Christian manner of slaughter adopted from the adherents of the *Alukta*, on the other hand, requires more courage on the part of the man facing the buffalo alone. Holding the animal weighing several hundred kilograms by a rope stringed through its nostrils, he must kill it with a single dash of the machete. The stroke in the throat, however, is not always powerful enough, and thus the buffalo often continues to suffer in agony for several more minutes, gasping for air, and even running about before ultimately collapsing.

Throughout the afternoon, further guests continued to arrive (in total they amounted to several hundred people) and were seated – as in other Toraja funerals – on bamboo platforms erected specifically for the purpose; they were welcomed with offerings of coffee, tea and cakes. After a meal (the fare was meat of the slaughtered buffaloes with vegetables and rice) the guests dispersed, marking the end of all activities related to the fortieth night. For Mrs. Nurhayati and her family, this was the last rite held to honour the death of her father.

3.5.3 The Slaughter of the Buffaloes

According to Mr. Bumbun Pakata, the majority of Muslims in the Toraja region slaughter buffaloes during death-related rituals; according to his estimate, approximately 60 % of the total number of Toraja Muslims. Some Islamic movements, for instance the Muhammadiyah[234] do not practice animal slaughter at all, while others like Nahdatul Ulama,[235] of which both Mr. Bumbun Pakata and Mrs. Nurhayati are members, sanction it. My respondent voiced the view that it was more appropriate for Muslims not to slaughter buffaloes, but should they do so, they have a full right to, being Toraja. On the other hand, he appreciated that traditional funerals bring the family together and cement solidarity among individual family members. Still, he stressed that it is most important that Muslims not borrow money for the purchase of buffaloes, as this is not in keeping with their religion. Mr. Bumbun Pakata used the very same argument as the Pentecostalist pastor Nehemia Tangkin when claiming that if someone has to borrow money, it is evident they are in a dire financial predicament further exacerbated by going into debt. In the course of our interview, Mr. Bumbun Pakata repeatedly emphasized that Islam as professed by the Toraja is no different than Islam as practised in other parts of Indonesia or the rest of the world, and that Muslim Toraja funerals are specific due to their combination of Islam and Toraja traditions. He further explained that the slaughter of animals is in no way related to the deceased, and that Muslims undertake this practice simply in order to be able to offer funeral guests a repast. Some Toraja want to continue these practices, but there are also objectors, and

---

234 Muhammadiyah is the second largest Indonesian Islamic organisation, associating a total of 29 million members. It was founded by the Muslim scholar Ahmad Dahlan in Yogyakarta in Central Java in 1912. It is not a political party but an organization whose activities focus primarily on the social sphere, in particular charity and education. In the religious sphere, they strive for the "purification" of Islam from local influences. It is thus only natural that they do not sanction the slaughter of buffaloes, which is obviously related to indigenous religion. The Toraja adherents of the Muhammadiyah movement in fact sometimes do not even celebrate subsequent funeral ceremonies (*malam pertama, malam kedua* and others), but merely bury the deceased.

235 Nahdatul Ulama (NU) is the largest Indonesian Islamic organisation, founded in 1926. The scope of its activities is comparable to Muhammadiyah, likewise focusing on the support of education and healthcare. Most of its adherents hail from the rural areas of Java. NU is far more tolerant of local influences which often determine the form of Islam existing in the given area.

thus feuds sometimes arise within family members. These disagreements may be caused, among other things, by their adherence to different movements of Islam. The following section features a transcript of my interview with Mrs. Nurhayati, who addresses this very issue.

3.5.4 Interview with Mrs. Nurhayati

Interview no. 8

Throughout the interview, Mrs. Nurhayati's husband was present, and at her bidding he also addressed some of my questions.

M. B.: How many buffaloes were slaughtered? [*It is clear from our previous discussion that I am inquiring as to the number of buffaloes sacrificed for the fortieth night ritual.*]

N.:[236] Eight.

M. B.: Who purchased them?

N.: I purchased six.

M. B.: Six? [*I have never before encountered a case where in a family of six children, one of them would sacrifice as many as six out of the total number of eight.*]

N.: Because two of my siblings did not want to take part in it. They did not want to take part in these customs.

M. B.: They didn't?

N.: They said that when he died, that was the end. We are Muslim, but we also practice Toraja customs. The Toraja kill buffaloes. [*This answer epitomises the ambivalent attitude of modern Toraja towards the buffalo sacrifices. The respondent stresses, that she is a Muslim, but on the other hand, she also feels to be a Toraja, and thus she endorses the custom.*]

M. B.: You personally feel that without the slaughter of the buffaloes, the ritual would be incomplete?

N.: Not that it would be incomplete but rather... how would I then feel? It is a token of respect for our parents, since we have money, but nobody is forcing us. It is all up to us, to our own will, if we really want to do this, to pay our parents the last respect and we happen to have the means, there is nothing wrong with having buffaloes slaughtered. And we slaughter them in order to provide food for the guests, in order to eat together, that's what it is. And yet some of my siblings did not want to take part in this.

---

236 Nurhayati.

M. B.: How many were they?

N.: Two did not want to participate. One is not married yet – he still has no commitments, doesn't have a job as yet, one died, and one, the eldest, is at Irian,[237] he did not participate. He just helped out a little.

M. B.: So he did not come?

N.: No, because he didn't have the means for the journey, he lives all the way in Papua.

M. B.: And there is another one?

N.: Yes, the one who had two buffaloes slaughtered.

M. B.: Did your father wish you to slaughter buffaloes after his death, or not? Or perhaps you did not speak about that?

N.: He addressed this at one point when he told his wife, my mother, if the children have money, let them kill seven buffaloes. If they can afford it... if they can't, well, there's nothing that can be done about that. This is what he told her, but he never forced us. For it is a kind of standard, you see they say that when... what do you call it? When you are above the common people... how is it with the caste now?

H.:[238] Well, that will be the middle caste.

N.: He once said he would wish for this, but he never forced us. He said, if the children can afford it, it would be good if they slaughter seven buffaloes. If they cannot, nobody will force them. Let them slaughter as many as they can afford.

M. B. And what reason did your two siblings give, those who wouldn't participate? Why wouldn't they?

N.: They said that if he is dead now, that is the end of that. He has already been buried.

[*I deliberately returned to the same question, for in the previous part of my interview my interlocutor touched upon the subject only briefly. I hoped to make her expand on the other reasons why her siblings would not participate in the financing and preparation of this ritual, but she gave me an almost identical answer to the previous one.*]

H.: They are adherents of another religious tendency.

N.: They are adherents of another religious tendency – it is still Islam, but modern Islam.

H.: What tendency is that? [*Based on my subsequent study of the issue at hand, I believe they were most likely adherents of Muhammadiyah.*]

---

237 The term "Irian" denotes one of the two Indonesian provinces that are today called Papua Barat (West Papua) and Papua. Both provinces lie in the west part of the island of New Guinea.

238 Husband.

N.: I don't want to speak about that as they do not wish it.

H.: I do not know what doctrine that is. [*I believe there was a misunderstanding here. I was asking about the name of the trend in Islam to which her siblings adhere, but Mrs. Nurhayati mistakenly assumed I wanted to discuss its characteristic features, something she evidently was not prepared to do.*]

N.: Only one would not participate. The other wanted to, but he is poor, the poor soul doesn't have any money. He has no money to contribute to buy even half a buffalo, or to help out, because indeed, he does not have a job. But as for that other one, he doesn't want any part in it.

H.: Because he is an adherent of another religious tendency, so we cannot say that he sinned or did any wrong, we cannot say that, for it is just different. It is his personal affair, he has his own view, it is difficult. It's hard to say whether he is wrong or right.

My interviewee likewise mentioned several reasons why, as a Muslim, she decided to make the buffalo sacrifice for her father. Foremost she cited that her Toraja identity is as important to her as her allegiance to Islam, and as a Toraja, she wanted to sacrifice the buffaloes. Another argument she cited – like many other Toraja who want to reassure themselves of the justness of their actions – was that the animals serve as a repast for the guests. Family solidarity and maintaining good relations with friends, neighbours and the community were always regarded of great importance, and as a result, she also stressed the social aspect of the occasion. She was convinced that by slaughtering the buffaloes, she paid final respects to her parent – no small factor in her decision to do so was that it had been her father's wish. I believe that the deceased family's fear of a negative reaction by the community should they refrain from practising this custom is also a rather strong motive for the slaughter of buffaloes.

Analyzing this interview, I was struck at first glance by how often my interviewee cited that nobody made her slaughter the buffaloes for her father. She stressed this fact five times in a few minutes. No less remarkable was her "selective" approach to her Toraja identity. Mrs. Nurhayati felt it was perfectly natural that as a Toraja she should make the buffalo sacrifice, yet the original significance of the act (the souls of the sacrificed animals transporting the soul of the deceased to *puya*) was not recognized by her, as in fact it is with most contemporary Toraja. She understood the slaughter of buffaloes merely as a symbol of her Toraja identity, without any religious connotations whatsoever. Although in the course of our interview, she never explicitly expressed disapproval, still there was an evident reproach of one of her siblings, who had refused to have any part of the buffalo sacrifice, ignoring their father's wishes. The economic aspect of the matter was probably also of considerable consequence, yet she made no reference to it. Given the circumstances, she and her husband were forced to bear the greatest part of the expense of the ritual on their own.

Based on the interviews I have undertaken as well as the results of my observation of the Muslim ritual cited, I came to the conclusion that Toraja Muslims struggle with the same predicament as Toraja Christians. They are constantly striving to find a reasonable compromise between the correct conduct of a true believer (a Muslim, in this case), and a good Toraja. I believe that although some Toraja profess to be adherents of Islam, their behaviour shows a clear effort to preserve their original traditions as derived from the *Alukta* religion. The customs of their ancestors, however, can be practised only when not in contradiction with Islam. Since their faith forbids the consumption of pork, in their version of the ritual, only buffaloes are sacrificed. Since Toraja Muslims must bury their dead within twenty-four hours, and it is naturally impossible to organize a funeral with all the characteristic Toraja attributes, the Muslim Toraja display their Toraja identity only during the rite of the fortieth night.

All contemporary Toraja funeral rites are unquestionably derived from the autochthonous religion. Their form, however, differs fundamentally depending to which religion the individuals performing these rites adhere to. The fewest elements of *Aluk Todolo* are found in the rites of Muslims and adherents of the Pentecostal Movement, and they are most abundant in the rites of the Catholics. Original *Alukta* funerals hardly occur at all at present.

4   Conclusion

The present work is an attempt to document the changes that Toraja society has undergone as a result of the arrival of Christian missionaries at the beginning of the 20th century in the territory of what is today Tana Toraja and Toraja Utara. I studied the shifts in the form and meaning of the traditional rituals on the currently most important ritual – the funeral. I inquired to what extent the present-day Toraja rituals are a syncretic phenomenon, combining the autochthonous belief system of *Aluk Todolo* and the customary law *adat* with newly adopted religions (various denominations of Christianity, and exceptionally also Islam), which play a major role in shaping the contemporary forms of ritual as well as of society at large. Based on analysis of the material gathered during my field research, my conclusions can be summed up in several basic points.

4.1   Transformation of Toraja Culture and Religion

Christianity, which first arrived in the Toraja region in 1913, was promoted non-violently and initially was embraced mainly by children attending Christian schools (the only existing educational institutions at the time), which were established by the missionaries immediately upon arrival. Parents as a rule learned about Christianity from their offspring, and sometimes also from the teachers themselves, who occasionally visited the families of pupils. Unlike their children, adults initially rejected Christianity; however, many also gradually converted, and in later years the Christian faith was passed from one generation to the next. Those of my respondents who converted to Christianity in childhood cited that – with Catholics in particular – an important factor in their conversion was their visual impression of the Christian rituals (they were impressed by the decoration of churches, as well as the ornate vestments of the priests), the sacral atmosphere present in the churches, and also the reading of captivating Biblical narratives. It may thus be concluded that the first Toraja to convert did so mostly due to the outward attractiveness of the new religion rather than for its essential content. At present, 89% of the total population of the Tana region claim to be Christian.

The adherents of the traditional belief system today are found mostly among members of the older generation. My research confirmed that young people have little interest in indigenous religion, perceiving it as a belief of their ancestors that no longer has anything to do with their lives, and so their notions of it are negligible and distorted. Authorities well-versed in Toraja culture and religion thus struggle with the essential problem that there is no one to pass this vast store of knowledge on to. Another factor hindering the preservation of the original faith is that unlike other religions, *Aluk Todolo* is not taught in schools.

Given the fact that adherents of the original religion form only 4% of the total population today, rituals performed in keeping with *Aluk Todolo* represent a rarity at present. They have been replaced by rituals where the influence of the newly adopted religions is visible. A vast majority of rites are palpably derived from *Aluk Todolo* and are merely supplemented by Christian (or, in rare cases, Muslim) elements – this shift is most pronounced in funeral rituals. Christians are vehemently opposed to this view, however, claiming that far from featuring elements of *Aluk Todolo,* their rituals in fact contain elements of the customary law *adat*. The roots of this argument go back to the latter half of the 20th century, when Christian priests and pastors developed a rather bizarre solution whereby they interpreted and presented Toraja culture on two levels: on one level the *adat* – an ancestral tradition which must be practiced and cultivated, and on the other *Aluk Todolo* – the original religion, regarded as obsolete and inappropriate – as a result of which it must be replaced by Christianity. Introducing this distinction allowed the Toraja to believe that they are contributing to the continuity of ancestral tradition while being practicing Christians. These facts clearly show that *Aluk Todolo* and its rituals in their original form will soon become completely extinct. However, deeply rooted customs in a modified form with added Christian elements will survive.

4.2   Funeral Rites

At first glance, contemporary funeral rites are very similar to the original *Aluk Todolo* rituals; on closer scrutiny, however, the shift in both form and meaning is evident. Christians no longer believe that the souls of the sacrificed animals will transport the soul of the deceased to the realm of *puya*, but nevertheless, they continue to sacrifice buffaloes and pigs. Since the meat of these animals is no longer used to prepare the *pesung* (offering), the main argument in support of the sacrifice is the duty to offer a repast to all funeral guests. However, as one of my respondents logically countered, if the Toraja really slaughtered animals only for food, they would no longer place such an extraordinary emphasis on their appearance – they would include female or handicapped animals (e.g. buffaloes with damaged horns or broken tails) in the killings, and would not be willing to spend up to 10,000 US dollars for a single buffalo. Based on the information I gathered, it can be stated that the sacrifice of animals during funeral rites is so deeply rooted in Toraja culture that the Toraja are unable to relinquish this custom which originated in their autochthonous religion even after adopting Christianity. They continue to perform this ceremony, absolutely essential for their culture, as is, even today, although they may no longer believe or understand the original purpose of the animal sacrifice.

As a result of Toraja society undergoing a transition from *Aluk Todolo* to Christianity, some religions and social functions were abolished and a portion of their roles transferred to other persons. The role of the ceremonial priests of *Aluk Todolo*, who in the past administered communication with God using the offerings (*pesung*), as well as the role of other persons performing activities related to rituals, was then taken on by Catholic or Protestant clergymen, or, in some cases, by members of the immediate family of the deceased. At present, many rites which form part of the funeral are performed in much the same way as in the past, but with a seminal shift in both meaning and purpose. In practicing contemporary rituals, Christian priests or pastors naturally do not invoke *Puang Matua* (God) or the *deata* (deities), praying instead to the Christian God; still, these ceremonies undeniably originate in *Aluk Todolo*. The Christians thus to some extent have preserved the form of the original funeral rituals, while fundamentally changing their meaning.

The tolerance of various religious denominations towards the inclusion of elements of the autochthonous religion differs rather greatly. Catholics are the most tolerant, allowing the practice of almost all customs originating in *Aluk Todolo*, while nevertheless re-evaluating their content. The strictest among the Christians are the Pentecostalists; with some Pentecostal denominations forbidding buffalo and pig sacrifices during funeral rites altogether. Toraja

Muslims are a unique group, since they bury their dead immediately after death, in keeping with Islamic prescripts, but they nevertheless still hold a ceremony forty days later similar to a Toraja funeral.

Social stratification was an important factor in the past, which used to absolutely determine the structure of the society, its functioning as well as the type of rituals that members of various social classes were allowed to practice. Since the second half of the 20th century, apart from social status, the financial means of the family of the deceased have also played a role. Even today, social status, to a large extent, determines the type of funeral that will be held (particularly in the south of the Toraja region), although it is no longer the sole determining factor.

In spite of considerable changes that have taken place in the performance of funerals, it can be concluded that at present, funeral rituals are as essential to Toraja society as they have been in the past, and to a large extend, they continue to play a vital role in their culture, in spite of the fact that the Toraja Christians are reluctant to admit this.

Summary

The present work is an attempt to analyse shifts in the form and meaning of the funeral rituals of the Toraja ethnic group, which have occurred due to the religious and social changes in Toraja society during the course of the 20th century. The seminal turning point which opened this hitherto closed socio-cultural system to external influences and which made the Toraja gradually relinquish their original belief and rituals was the arrival of Dutch Christian missionaries in 1913. My field research proved that traditional Toraja rituals in their autochthonous form are all but extinct in the Toraja region; but they were nevertheless replaced by new forms which are derived from these rituals, but include elements of Christianity (and in some unique cases of Islam). In terms of funeral rituals, some minor changes occurred in terms of form, while the changes in terms of content were substantial.

One may only guess whether the rapid and essential shift in the practice of rituals, which in this case occurred as a result of the arrival of a new religion, may be symptomatic of cultures whose traditions are not codified as heritage in the form of written literature. I believe that the indigenous traditions of such ethnic groups fall prey more easily to the power of attractive and "civilized" cultures, and as a result, are subject to irreversible and fundamental change.

Bibliography

Alkitab [The Bible] (2006): Lembaga Alkitab Indonesia, Jakarta.

Adams, K. (1993): Club Dead, Not Club Med: Staging Death in Contemporary Tana Toraja, *Southeast Asian Journal of Social Science* 21 (2), pp. 62–72.

Adams, K. (1998): Domestic Tourism and National-Building in South Sulawesi, *Indonesia and the Malay World* 26 (75), pp. 77–96.

Adams, K. (2003): The Politics of Heritage in Tana Toraja, Indonesia: Interplaying the Local and the Global, *Indonesia and the Malay World* 31 (89), pp. 91–107.

Bigalke, T. W. (2005): *Tana Toraja: A Social History of an Indonesian People.* Koninklijk Institut voor Taal-, Land- en Volkenkunde, Leiden.

Budil, I. T. (1999): *Mýtus, jazyk a kulturní antropologie* [Myth, Language and Cultural Anthropology]. Triton, Praha.

Budil, I. T. (2001): *Za obzor západu* [Beyond the Horizons of the West]. Triton, Praha.

Budiman-Rybková, M. – Lorencová, R. (2010): Torajské pohřební rituály a vliv sociální stratifikace na jejich podobu [Toraja Funeral Rituals and the Impact of Social Stratification on Their Form], *Studia Ethnologica Pragensia* 1, pp. 69–81.

Budiman, M. (2010): Torajské funerální rituály v minulosti a současnosti [Toraja Funeral Rituals in the Past and Present], *Studia Ethnologica Pragensia* 2, pp. 93–104.

Budiman, M. (2011): Toradžští pentekostalisté a jejich pohřby [Toraja Pentecostalists and Their Funerals], *Studia Ethnologica Pragensia* 1, pp. 87–97.

Budiman, M. (2011): Přijímání křesťanství mezi Toradži [Conversion to Christianity Among the Toraja], *Studia Ethnologica Pragensia* 2, pp. 137–144.

Budiman, M. (2011): The Buffalo in the Culture of the Toraja Ethnic Group of Sulawesi, Indonesia, *Pandanus '11* 5 (1), pp. 7–22.

Budiman, M. (2012): The Influence of Christianity on the Form and Understanding of Funeral Rituals in the Toraja Ethnic Group of Sulawesi, Indonesia, *Pandanus '12* 6 (1), pp. 65–78.

Crystal, E. (1974): Cooking Pot Politics: A Toraja Village Study, *Indonesia* 18. Southeast Asia Program Publications at Cornell University, Ithaca, pp. 118–151.

Crystal, E. (1978): Tourism in Toraja (Sulawesi, Indonesia). *Hosts and Guests – The Anthropology of Tourism.* Editor Smith, V. L. Basil Blackwell, Oxford, pp. 109–125.

Dubovská, Z. (1973): Lodě zemřelých duší [Ships for the Departed Souls], *Nový Orient* 6, pp. 169–171.

Dubovská, Z. – Petrů, T. – Zbořil, Z. (2005): *Dějiny Indonésie* [The History of Indonesia]. Nakladatelství Lidové noviny, Praha.

Eliade, M. (1959): *The Sacred and the Profane: The Nature of Religion*. Harcourt, New York.

Van den End, Th. (1994): *Sumber-sumber Zending tentang Sejarah Gereja Toraja 1901–1961* [Missionary Sources Regarding the History of the Toraja Protestant Church]. Pt Bpk Gunung Mulia, Jakarta.

Endang, N. Y. – Gunawan, A. et al. (1984): *Upacara Tradisional (Upacara Kematian) Daerah Sulawesi Selatan* [Traditional Rituals (funeral rituals) in the Region of South Sulawesi]. Jakarta.

Ensiklopedi Nasional Indonesia [Indonesian National Encyclopaedia] (1988): Pt Cipta Adi Pustaka 16, Jakarta.

Frazer, J. G. (1996): *The Golden Bough. A Study in Magic and Religion*. Penguin, London.

Geertz, C. (1973): *The Interpretation of Cultures; Selected Essays*. Basic Books, New York.

Van Gennep, A. (1960): *The Rites of Passage*. University of Chicago Press, Chicago.

Ghozi Badrie, H. M. (1997): *Aluk Todolo dan Tradisi Simpan Mayat di Tana Toraja* [Aluk Todolo and the Traditions of Preserving the Deceased in Tana Toraja]. Gunung Pesagi Bandar Lampung, Bandar Lampung.

Halík, T. (2006): *Prolínání světů: ze života světových náboženství.* [Intersecting Worlds: From the Life of World Religions]. Nakladatelství Lidové noviny, Praha.

The Holy Bible. King James Version.

Kabanga', A. (2002): *Manusia Mati Seutuhnya: Suatu Kajian Antropologi Kristen* [People Die Entirely: A Christian Study in Anthropology]. Media Pressindo, Yogyakarta.

Kabanga', A. – Mangoting, A. (2002): *Menabur dan Melayani* [Sermon and Service]. Rantepao.

Kennedy, R. (1974): *Bibliography of Indonesian People and Culture*. Southeast Asia Studies Yale University by arrangement with Human Relations Area Files, New Haven.

Kobong, Th. et al. (1992): *Aluk, Adat dan Kebudayaan Toraja dalam Perjumpaannya dengan Injil* [Aluk, Custom Law and Toraja Culture Confronted with the Holy Bible]. Institut Theologia Indonesia, Jakarta.

Kobong, Th. – Lebang, J. et al. (1994): *Iman dan Kebudayaan* [Faith and Culture]. Gunung Mulia, Jakarta.

Kobong, Th. – Lebang, J. et al.: *Roh-roh dan Kuasa-kuasa Gaib* [Spirits and Supernatural Powers]. Institut Theologia Gereja Toraja.

Kudělka, V. (1983): *Malý labyrint literatury* [Encyclopaedia of Literature]. Československý spisovatel, Praha.

Lévi-Strauss, C. (1967): *Structural Anthropology*. Anchor Books, Garden City, N. Y.

Lévi-Strauss, C. (1966): *The Savage Mind*. University of Chicago Press, Chicago.

Lévi-Strauss, C. (1963): *Totemism*. Beacon Press, Boston.

Liku Ada', J. (1986): *Towards a Spirituality of Solidarity*. Dissertation. Roma.

Lužný, D. (1999): *Náboženství a moderní společnost. Sociologická teorie modernizace a sekularizace* [Religion and Modern Society. A Sociological Theory of Modernization and Secularization]. Masarykova univerzita, Brno.

Manta', Y.: *Fenomenologi Adat – Budaya dan Kepercayaan Asli Toraja* [The Phenomenology of Custom Law – Culture and Original Toraja Religion]. Tana Toraja.

Manta', Y. (1991): *Perkawinan Adat Toraja* [Traditional Toraja Weddings], *SAWI* 5, pp. 183–200.

Manusia Toraja: dari mana – bagaimana – ke mana [The Toraja: Where From – How – Where To] (1983): Institut Theologia Gereja Toraja.

Marampa', A. T., – Labuhari, U. (1997): *Budaya Toraja* [Toraja Culture]. Yayasan Maraya, Jakarta.

Marampa', A. T. (1974): *Guide to Tana Toraja*. Rantepao.

Marampa', A. T. (1981): *Mengenal Toraja* [Meet the Toraja].

Munoz, P. M. (2006): *Early Kingdoms of the Indonesian Archipelago and the Malay Peninsula*. Didier Millet, Singapore.

Murphy, R. F. (1986): *Cultural and Social Anthropology: An Overture*. Prentice Hall, Englewood Cliffs, N. J.

Nooy-Palm, H. (1975): Introduction to the Sa'dan Toraja People and Their Country, *Archipel*. Association Archipel, Paris, pp. 53–91.

Nooy-Palm, H. (1979): *The Sa'dan-Toraja: A Study of Their Social Life and Religion I. Organization, Symbols and Believes*. Koninklijk Institut voor Taal-, Land- en Volkenkunde, Leiden.

Nooy-Palm, H. (1986): *The Sa'dan-Toraja: A Study of Their Social Life and Religion II. Rituals of the East and West*. Foris, Dordrecht.

Oplt, M. (1989): *Hledání Indonésie* [In Search of Indonesia]. Panorama, Praha.

Paranoan, M. N. (1994): *Rambu Solo' Upacara Kematian Orang Toraja: Analisis Psiko – Sosio – Kultural* [Smoke Descending Rituals – Toraja Funeral Rituals: a Psychological, Social and Cultural Analysis]. SULO, Rantepao.

Parinding, S. C. et al. (1988): *Toraja Indonesia's Mountain Eden*. Times Editions, Singapore.

Robson, S. – Kurniasih, Y. (2010): *Basic Indonesian*. Tuttle Publishing, Singapore.

Salombe', C. (1972): *Orang Toraja dengan Rithusnya* [The Toraja and Their Rituals]. Frater, Ujung Pandang.

Said, A. A. (2004): *Simbolisme Unsur Visual Rumah Tradisional Toraja* [The Symbolism of Visual Elements on Traditional Toraja Houses]. Ombak, Yogyakarta.

N'ha Sandra, J. (1998): From "You Toradja" to "We Toraya", *A Journal of the Southeast Asian Studies Student Association* 2 (1), pp. 1–17.

Sandarupa, S. (1984): *Life and Death of the Toraja People*. Gemini Mulia, Rantepao.

Sandarupa, S. (2000): *Life And Death in Toraja*. 21 Computer, Ujung Pandang.

Sarira, Y. A. (1996): *Rambu Solo' dan Persepsi Orang Kristen tentang Rambu Solo'* [Funeral Rituals and Their Perception by Christians]. Pusbang Gereja Toraja.

Van Schie, G. (2000): *Gereja Katolik di Tana Toraja dan Luwu: Sejarah tentang Awal Perkembangannya* [The History of the Early Development of the Catholic Church in Tana Toraja and Luwu]. OBOR, Jakarta.

Van Schie, G. (2003): *Gereja Katolik di Toraja Barat: Sejarah tentang Awal Perkembangannya* [The History of the Early Development of the Catholic Church in Toraja Barat]. Pandu Dewanata Abadi, Jakarta.

Sitonda, M. N. (2005): *Toraja Warisan Dunia* [Toraja World Heritage]. Pustaka Refleksi, Makassar.

Soukup, V. (1999): *Přehled antropologických teorií kultury* [A Survey of Anthropological Theories of Culture]. Portál, Praha.

Steiner, F. B. (1999): *Tabu, Truth, and Religion*. Berghahn Books, New York.

Swellengrebel, J. L. (1978): In Memoriam Dr. Hendrik van der Veen. *Bijdragen tot de Taal-, Land- en Volkenkunde (BKI)* [Journal of the Humanities and Social Sciences of Southeast Asia and Oceania] 134. Koninklijk Institut voor Taal-, Land- en Volkenkunde,'s-Gravenhage.

Tammu, J. – van der Veen, H. (1971): *Kamus Toraja–Indonesia* [Toraja – Indonesian Dictionary]. Yayasan Perguruan Kristen Toraja, Jakarta.

Tana Toraja dalam Angka [Tana Toraja Regency in Figures], (2005). Rantepao.

Tangdilintin, L. T. (1985): *Tongkonan (Rumah Adat Toraja): Arsitektur & Ragam Hias Toraja* [Tongkonan (Traditional Toraja House): Architecture & Toraja Decoration]. Yayasan Lepongan Bulan, Tana Toraja.

Tangdilintin, L. T. (1975): *Toraja dan Kebudayaannya* [The Toraja and Their Culture]. Yayasan Lepongan Bulan, Tana Toraja.

Tangdilintin, L. T. (1980): *Upacara Pemakan Adat Toraja* [Traditional Toraja Funerals]. Yayasan Lepongan Bulan, Tana Toraja.

Tsintjilonis, D. (1997): Embodied Difference: The 'Body-Person' of the Sa'dan Toraja, *Bijdragen tot de Taal-, Land- en Volkenkunde (BKI)* [Journal of the Humanities and Social Sciences of Southeast Asia and Oceania]. Koninklijk Institut voor Taal-, Land- en Volkenkunde, Leiden, pp. 244–272.

Tsintjilonis, D. (2000): A Head for the Dead: Sacred Violence in Tana Toraja, *Archipel 59*. Association Archipel, Paris, pp. 27–50.

Tsintjilonis, D. (2000): Death and Sacrifice of Signs: Measuring the Dead in Tana Toraja, *Oceania* 71. Southwood Press, Sydney, pp. 1–17.

Vodáková, A. – Vodáková, O. et al. (2000): *Sociální a kulturní antropologie* [Social and Cultural Anthropology]. SLON, Praha.

Volkman, T. A. (1980): *The Pig Has Eaten the Vegetables: Ritual and Change in Tana Toraja*. Dissertation. Ann Arbor.

Volkman, T. A. (1984): Great Performances: Toraja Cultural Identity in the 1970s, *American Ethnologist* 11. American Ethnological Society, Arlington, pp. 152–169.

Volkman, T. A. (1986): *Feasts of Honor: Ritual and Change in the Toraja Highlands*. University of Illinois Press, Urbana and Chicago.

Volkman, T. A. (1990): Visions and Revisions: Toraja Culture and the Tourist Gaze, *American Ethnologist* 17. American Ethnological Society, Arlington, pp. 91–110.

Waterson, R. (1984): *Ritual and Belief Among the Sa'dan Toraja: Two Studies*. University of Kent, Canterbury.

Waterson, R. (1993): Taking the Place of Sorrow: The Dynamics of Mortuary Rites among the Sa'dan Toraja, *Southeast Asian Journal of Social Science* 21 (2), pp. 73–96.

Waterson, R. (1995): Graves and the Limits of Kinship Groupings among the Sa'dan Toraja, *Bijdragen tot de Taal-, Land- en Volkenkunde (BKI)* [Journal of the Humanities and Social Sciences of Southeast Asia and Oceania]. Koninklijk Institut voor Taal-, Land- en Volkenkunde, Leiden, pp. 194–217.

Appendices

Transcription of Interviews in Indonesian

Interview no. 1

M. B.:[239] Dan, setelah upacara selesai, daun dan pinang bisa dimakan oleh orang?

T. D.:[240] Bisa, bisa. Pada biasanya orang-orang hamil, kalau mau cantik, makan sesajen, kalau anaknya mau cantik, makan.

M. B.: Sesajen daun sirih dan pinang atau yang nasi, ayam?

T. D.: Nasi, ayam, jadi dimakan kalau ada orang hamil, oknum yang hamil. Pernah dulu saya katakan pada seorang anak, di apa, ya, di Enrekang, saya buat ini, acara semacam begini. Kebetulan oknumnya hitam-hitam, istri dari kemenakan saya, saudaranya yang hamil, itu oknumnya hitam, dia kan orang Flores, suaminya pun orang Flores, hitam-hitam. Saya panggil dia, "Eh, mari kau, saya kasi *pesung* supaya anakmu nanti jadi putih-putih." Dia ragu, dia bilang, "Bisakah?". "Kenapa tidak?" Setelah lahir anaknya, ribut dia di rumah sakit, gara-gara putih seperti bangsa Barat, seperti kita-kita ini. Dia bilang, "Lahir Belanda gara-gara Nene' Tato'." [*Tertawa.*] Ah, anak itu, ya, tangkas, bahkan ndak mau kalah. Jadi, entah sekarang sudah masuk SD, tapi dia selalu cari-cari saya. Waktunya pertama kali datang, "Saya mau cium Nene' Sando, di mana dia?" Terus saya dipeluk-peluk, "Gara-gara saya cantik, karena kamu. Itu sebabnya saya cantik." [*Tertawa.*]

Interview no. 2

M. B.: Waktu itu kalau mau sekolah, harus bayar?

P. T. R. A.:[241] Ya, bayar. Waktu itu saya punya nenek di Makale, waktu mau bayar uang sekolah harus pergi ke kantor nenek di Makale, bawa surat minta uang sekolah. Uang sekolahnya dua puluh lima sen.

---

239 Michaela Budiman.
240 Tato' Dena'.
241 Puang Toding Rante Allo.

M. B.: Dua puluh lima sen per bulan?

P. T. R. A.: Ya, per bulan.

M. B.: Kalau mau beli umpamanya satu kilo beras, berapa harganya waktu itu?

P. T. R. A.: Murah, itu masih murah. Waktu kita punya orang tua, masih murah, belum banyak orang. Kalau ada lima orang di rumah, itu sudah banyak.

M. B.: Tapi kalau mau beli satu kilo beras harganya berapa?

P. T. R. A.: Murah.

M. B.: Saya ingin tahu itu supaya saya bisa membayangkan berapa itu dibandingkan dengan uang sekolah.

P. T. R. A.: Kita tidak pernah beli beras, tanam sendiri.

M. B.: Kalau mau beli seekor kerbau harganya berapa?

P. T. R. A.: Seratus lima puluh sen. Kita tidak perlu beli beras, kita tidak tahu harganya, kita punya beras sendiri.

Interview no. 3

M. B.: Tapi bagaimana perasaan ibu? Karena pasti di rumah dan di kampung semua masih *Alukta* dan ada acara *Alukta* dan nanti di sekolah ada sesuatu yang lain yang diajar. Bagaimana perasaan?

M. P.:[242] Saya memang sudah buang itu adat-adat anu. Saya pegang sama Kristen, saya tertarik. Tadi bapakku orang *adat* itu tapi dia tidak marah sama sekali. Kalau ibuku jengkel. Tetapi dia bilang, "Ah, tidak boleh dimarahi itu anak. Apa dia suka, jangan dianu." Bagus juga!

Interview no. 4

J. L.:[243] Dan ketiga bapak itu hari, tiga hari, karena memang karena agak mendadak, terburu-buru maksudnya, tiga hari sebelum pesta dimulai kita sudah rapat.

M. B.: Kenapa terburu-buru? Kenapa mau mengubur cepat?

J. L.: Begini, kita mau kubur cepat karena kebetulan bapak sudah meninggalnya di Makassar atau dengan kata lain yang nama lain Ujung Pandang dan kita sudah melaksanakan ibadah di sana sesuai dengan keyakinan kita dari Gereja Protestan dan di mana bapak atau almarhum terdaftar di Makassar sebagai salah satu anggota Gereja Toraja. Jadi, Protestan dan acaranya di sana sudah selesai, jadi di sana tinggal pelepasan jenazah dari Makassar sampai ke Tana Toraja. Dan kebetulan kita punya saudara, ia orang terikat, artinya bekerja di bidang pemerintahan yang tidak boleh sembarang mengambil waktu, artinya tidak bebas, karena mereka terikat dari pemerintah, itu sebabnya kita …. Dan yang kedua, secara jujur saja, kita mengakui dan harus saya katakan karena, ya, kemampuan dari ekonomi, ya, itu. Karena semakin lama di atas rumah, semakin banyak biaya, jadi, kita secepatnya melakukan karena, ya, itu tadi saya katakan karena keterbatasan ekonomi, ya, secara jujur. Walaupun sebenarnya bapak itu bisa kita pestakan berapa hari di belakang atau kapan, bisa kita, tidak ada masalah sebenarnya, cuma, ya, itu, masalah ekonomi. Dipercepat karena di Makassar kita sudah mengeluarkan banyak biaya. Di mana lagi kalau masih mau lama di Toraja? Tambah beban.

Interview no. 5

M. B.: Dan kira-kira berapa babi dipotong?

J. L.:[244] Aduh, sebenarnya saya kurang bisa anu … seandainya Mísa …. Buku itu, catatan ada sama saya, jadi di situ ditulis …

---

242 Martha Pudi.
243 Juchri Layuksugi.
244 Juchri Layuksugi.

M. B.: Tapi kira-kira?

J. L.: Karena tidak terlalu, kita juga tidak terlalu ini, apa, kita perhitungkan faktor ekonomi, pemborosan, jadi .... Sekitar lima puluh.

M. B.: Itu cukup, itu cukup banyak lima puluh.

Interview no. 6

M. B.: Apakah menurut bapak mengeluarkan banyak uang di upacara kematian adalah hal yang benar?

T. D.:[245] Jadi, pada biasanya begitu, jangan terlalu menghambur-hambur harta. Banyak gunanya, banyak kegunaannya, pakai membangun. Apalagi dalam dunia modern ini, biaya anak-anak. Ya, bisa membangun perdagangan, bisa membeli sawah, dan lain-lain. Bahkan, mengolah tanah yang masih kosong di daerah trans. Jadi, ada juga enaknya, ya. Modal untuk perdagangan, modal untuk pendidikan, modal untuk bisnis yang lain, membuka proyek, dan lain-lain.

Interview no. 7

Y. P.:[246] Di dalam pemotongan hewan ini, itu ada unsur-unsur pemborosan. Sekarang satu ekor kerbau belang itu seratus juta lebih, seratus sepuluh, seratus dua puluh juta! Satu ekor! Jadi itu bukan untuk lauk saja. Jadi, berlaku orang Kristen juga, di Katolik Toraja dan ada aliran Pantekosta, juga ada berapa yang masih memotong begitu. Tapi kalau ke gereja mana berani mau kasih seratus juta.

M. B.: Ya.

Y. P.: Kerbau kan dari Tuhan, Tuhan yang ciptakan, Tuhan yang kasih nafas, Tuhan yang tumbuhkan rumput, tapi kita potong untuk orang mati. Tapi ini bukan sekedar lauk. Kalau sekedar lauk-paukan, ah, kita beli saja yang jelek. Ya, kerbau, ya, betina yang sudah tidak beranak, tapi orang, di sini, orang tidak mau itu, mau potong begitu. Tanduknya yang rusak, ekornya yang putus, mereka tidak mau potong begitu. Jadi, kita yakini bahwa masih ada kaitannya dengan orang mati. Itu yang saya tulis di skripsi saya bahwa itu orang mati mempengaruhi orang hidup sehingga dia rela memboroskan harta bendanya untuk orang mati. Kalau sudah tidak ada hubungannya dengan orang mati, sebenarnya ndak ada masalahnya, no problem. Seperti di Manado, di Jawa, Jakarta, kalau ada orang mati, potong babi, potong sapi, ndak ada larangan, ndak ada hubungan dengan orang mati, memang untuk lauk saja. Tapi di sini bukan sekitar untuk lauk, ada buktinya. Itu dari segi nilai kerbaunya, nilai babinya. Babi juga tidak sembarang dibawa, tidak bawa yang betina, musti jantan. Apa orang mati musti tolak betina? Daging jantan betina kan sama saja enaknya. Tapi kenapa harus pilih begitu? Itu asalnya dari agama dulu.

Interview no. 8

M. B.: Berapa kerbau dipotong?

N.:[247] Delapan.

M. B.: Siapa yang beli kerbau itu?

N.: Yang beli kerbau, saya enam.

M. B.: Enam?!

N.: Karena ada saudara saya tidak mau ikut-ikut begitu. Ada saudara saya dua tidak mau ikut yang *adat* begitu.

M. B.: Tidak mau?

---

245 Tato' Dena'.
246 Yunus Padang.
247 Nurhayati.

N.: Katanya, kalau meninggal, ya, sudah. Tapi kita ini Muslim tapi ada juga ikut-ikut adat Toraja, ya. Orang Toraja kan potong-potong kerbau.

M. B.: Untuk anda sendiri perasaan kalau kerbau tidak dipotong merasa tidak lengkap?

N.: Bukan namanya tidak lengkap, tapi artinya merasa bagaimana, ya? Pengabdian untuk orang tua karena ada rezeki, tidak ada pemaksaan, tidak ada pemaksaan, itu semua tergantung sama kita, keikhlasan kita, kalau memang kita ikhlas, merasa pengabdian terakhir untuk orang tua, kebetulan ada rezeki, ya, tidak salah kalau kita potong. Dan kita potong untuk tamu – makan, tamu kan, kita potongkan untuk makan bersama, begitu, ya. Dan sementara yang saudara saya tidak mau ikut-ikut begitu.

M. B.: Berapa tidak mau ikut?

N.: Dua orang tidak mau ikut begitu. Satu belum nikah – itu tidak ada beban, ji, tidak ada pekerjaan, satu meninggal, satu yang paling sulung itu, ada di Irian, tidak ikut itu. Cuma bantu sedikit.

M. B.: Dan dia tidak datang?

N.: Tidak datang, karena tidak ada dana untuk biaya datang, dia jauh sekali di Papua.

M. B.: Dan satu lagi?

N.: Satu lagi, ya, itu yang potong dua ekor.

M. B.: Sebelum bapak meninggal ia mau supaya kalau sudah meninggal kerbau dipotong atau ia tidak mau atau anda tidak bicara tentang itu?

N.: Ya, ia pernah pesan, katanya sama isterinya, mama saya, kalau ada rezekinya anak, biar dipotongkan tujuh ekor. Kalau ada, kalau tidak ada, ya, apa boleh buat! Pesannya cuma begitu, tidak ada pemaksaan. Karena standarnya itu, standar katanya kalau … apa namanya? Di atas orang biasalah, begitu. Bagaimana anunya itu, pak, istilahnya kalau kasta?

S.:[248] Kalau itu, sudah kasta menengah.

N.: Jadi, memang pernah dia minta, itu pun tidak dipaksa. Dia bilang, kalau ada rezekinya kita punya anak sebaiknya dia potong sampai tujuh. Kalau tidak ada, tidak dipaksa juga. Berapa-berapa saja.

M. B.: Dan dua saudara itu yang tidak mau ikut mereka bilang apa? Kenapa tidak mau ikut?

N.: Katanya sudah, kalau sudah meninggal, ya, sudah. Dikubur itu.

S.: Aliran lain itulah.

N.: Aliran lain, Islam tapi Islam yang modern barangkali.

M. B.: Islam apa?

N.: Islam, apa yang tidak mau sebut, ya. Karena mereka tidak mau itu.

S.: Saya ndak tahu ajarannya.

N.: Cuma satu yang tidak mau ikut. Yang satu itu ikut tapi miskin, tidak punya dana, kasihan. Artinya tidak ada kasih masuk-masuk apakah beli kerbau setengah, atau bantuannya untuk saya tidak ada karena memang ia tidak punya pekerjaan. Kalau itu yang satu memang total tidak mau ikut yang begini.

S.: Karena sudah lain aliran, jadi kita nggak bisa bicara bahwa dia dosa atau dia salah, nggak bisa karena aliran lain. Ia punya pribadi, dia punya pendapat sendiri, jadi susah. Susah kita mau mengetahui bahwa dia yang salah atau dia yang benar.

---

248 Suami.

Main Informants

The age (in 2006) gender and education (although I did not establish the latter in all cases), profession, religion, and time and place of the interview are cited with regard to each informant. Grammar school (SD – Sekolah Dasar) takes six years in Indonesia, followed by three years of junior secondary school (SMP – Sekolah Menengah Pertama), and this in turn is followed by three years of senior secondary school (SMA – Sekolah Menengah Atas).

1. **Tato' Dena'**, male, age 69, grammar school and two years of junior secondary school, tominaa and tomenani, Aluk Todolo, Mandetek, April and May 2006.
2. **Drs. Lucas Paliling, Lic.IC**, male, age 51, university education, Catholic priest, Rantepao, January – May 2006.
3. **Drs. Stanislaus A. Dammen, MPS, MA.**, male, age 51, university education, Catholic priest, Rantepao, To' Pao, January – May 2006.
4. **Drs. Yohanes Manta' Rumengan**, male, age 45, university education, Catholic priest, Rantepao, To' Pao, February – May 2006.
5. **Paulus Pasang Kanan**, male, age 70, university education, secondary school teacher, retired, Salu Allo, March 24, 2006.
6. **Drs. Paulus Palondongan, MM**, male, age 36, university education, university lecturer, Catholic, Rantepao, January – May 2006.
7. **Hendra**, male, age 33, Aluk Todolo, Mandetek, April 2006. Note: son of Tato' Dena'.
8. **Rimba**, male, age cca 50, Catholic, Mandetek, May 2006. Note: relative of Tato' Dena'.
9. **Elisabeth Sau'Datuan**, female, age 66, housewife, Catholic, Sangalla', February 2006.
10. **Duma' Rante Tasik**, male, age 65, farmer, Protestant – Pentecostalist, Tonga, March 7, 2006.
11. **Yustina Limbong Allo**, female, age 34, housewife, Catholic, Tonga, March 7, 2006. Note: daughter of Duma' Rante Tasik.
12. **Samuel Minggu**, male, age 64, farmer, Catholic, Tampo Makale, February 19, 2006.
13. **Juchri Layuksugi**, male, age 38, farmer, Protestant, Rantepao, April 7, 2006.
14. **Herman Remang Rante Tandung**, male, age 31, university education, secondary school teacher, Catholic, Rantepao, March 2006.
15. **Kassa' Rante Allo**, male, age 46, community leader, Aluk Todolo, Lembang Tallung Penanian, March 19, 2006, March 26, 2006, April 9, 2006.

16. **Yulita Pindan Tangkeallo**, female, age 42, public education worker in the area of agriculture, Catholic, Lembang Tallung Penanian, March 19, 2006, March 26, 2006. Note: wife of Kassa' Rante Allo.
17. **Nene Joksi**, male, age 50, farmer, Aluk Todolo, Lembang Tallung Penanian, April 1, 2006.
18. **Lusiana Suka'**, female, age 64, shaman, housewife, Catholic, Tampo Makale, April 16, 2006.
19. **Efrain Padindik**, male, age 51, high-ranking police officer, Seventh-day Adventist, Makale, April 12, 2006.
20. **Ir. Robby Paliling**, male, age 29, university education, engineer, Catholic, Makassar, February and May 2006. Note: brother of Father Lucas Paliling.
21. **Yulianus Roge Paliling**, male, age 21, secondary school education, student at the Rantepao Catechetic and Pastoral Institute (STIKPAR), Catholic, Rantepao, January – May 2006. Note: cousin of Father Lucas Paliling.
22. **Nova Paliling**, female, age 18, secondary school education, student at the Healthcare Academy Rantepao (Akademi Kebidanan Rantepao), Catholic, Rantepao, January – May 2006. Note: cousin of Father Lucas Paliling.
23. **Alde Aldegonda**, female, age 20, secondary school education, student at the Rantepao Catechetic and Pastoral Institute (STIKPAR), Catholic, Rantepao, January – May 2006.
24. **Febri**, female, age 19, secondary school education, student at the Rantepao Catechetic and Pastoral Institute (STIKPAR), Catholic, Rantepao, January – May 2006.
25. **Lily**, female, age 53, housewife, Catholic, Rantepao, March and May 2006.
26. **Petrus Pangi**, male, age 19, secondary school education, student at the Rantepao Catechetic and Pastoral Institute (STIKPAR), Catholic, Rantepao, January – May 2006.
27. **Yasinta Rumengan Ronting**, female, age 62, grammar school teacher, retired, Catholic, To' Pao, May 5, 2006.
28. **Martha Pudi**, female, age 78, housewife, Protestant, To' Pao, May 9, 2006.
29. **Abigail Gali Payungallo**, female, age 78, housewife, Protestant, To' Pao, May 9, 2006.
30. **Gisberta Balla Tandiayu'**, female, age 66, nurse, Catholic, To' Pao, May 9, 2006.
31. **Puang Toding Rante Allo**, female, age 77, housewife, Catholic, To' Pao, May 9, 2006.
32. **Yunus Padang, STh.**, male, age 62, university education, pastor – Pentecostalist, Rantepao, April 30, 2006.
33. **Nehemia Tangkin, Sm. Th.**, male, age 39, university education, pastor – Pentecostalist, Bolu, April 21, 2006.

34. **Saarah Salino, Sm. Th.**, female, age 38, university education, Pentecostalist preacher, Bolu, April 21, 2006. Note: wife of Nehemia Tangkin.
35. **Nurhayati**, female, age 46, housewife, Muslim, Rantepao, April 20, 2006.
36. **Drs. H. Bumbun Pakata, MAg.**, male, age 58, university education, public servant – employee of the Ministry of Religion, Muslim, Rantepao, April 19, 2006.
37. **Drs. Arifuddin**, male, age 38, university education, public servant, employee of the Ministry of Religion in Makale, Muslim, Makale, April 12, 2006.
38. **Rafika Adriana L.A**, female, age 24, university education, public servant, Muslim, Rantepao, beginning of February 2006.
39. **Tulak Datu Allo**, female, age 45, housewife, Muslim, Rantepao, beginning of February 2006.

Timetable of the Funeral of Yohana Maria Sumbung

(distributed at the funeral among the guests)

UPACARA PEMAKAMAN ALMH. YOHANA MARIA SUMBUNG
TONGKONAN TO'PAO – LAMPIO, SANGALLA' – TANA TORAJA

WAKTU			NAMA – ACARA		KEGIATAN		PEN-TJ	KET
HARI	TGL	JAM	ADAT	LITURGI	ADAT	LITURGI		
KAMIS	4 MEI	SORE	Mangissi Lantang					
		18:00		Doa Keluarga			P. Stanis Dammen	
JUMAT	5 MEI	10:00	Ma'pasa' Tedong		Semua tedong masuk halaman		Sie Adat – Acara	
		14:00	Ma'karu'dusan		Potong dua kerbau		Sie Adat – Daging	
		17:00		Ibadat Pembuka		Doa diurus oleh Stasi	Desta Bun-Sal	
SABTU	6 MEI	09:00	Manombon		Mangriyu' batu, Ma' pabendan simbuang / bala'kayan, dll.		Sie Adat – Acara Siemanombon	
		10:00		Ibadat Rante	Potong satu kerbau	Ibadat di halaman sebelum berkati simbuang dan tedong.	Sie Liturgi P. John Manta'	
		15:00	Mellao alang		Jenasah diantar ke Lumbung		Sie Adat – Acara	
MINGGU	7 MEI		Ditorroi	Doa Keluarga				
		21:00					Sr. Yulitha Dammen	
SENIN	8 MEI	08:00	Ma' tombi		Persiapan		Keluarga	
		09:00			Ma'badong		Sie Pa'badong	

WAKTU			NAMA – ACARA		KEGIATAN		PEN-TJ	KET
HARI	TGL	JAM	ADAT	LITURGI	ADAT	LITURGI		
		11:00			Istirahat		Keluarga	
		12:05	Ma'pasonglo'		Perarakan mulai		Sie Ma'pasonglo'	
		14:00			Jenazah di Lakkian, Potong dua tedong		Sie Protokol Sie Adat – Daging	
		15:00			Terima Tamu		Sie Terima Tamu	
		16:30			Ma'pasilaga		Sie Adat – Acara	
		18:00		Ibadat Bersama			P. John Manta'	
SELASA	9 MEI	09:00	Mantunu: Terima Tamu		Potong tiga kerbau Manta Padang		Sie Adat – Daging Sie Adat / Protokol	
		12:30		Doa Makan			P. Nathan Runtung	
RABU	10 MEI	09:00	Mantunu: Terima Tamu		Potong empat kerbau		Sie Adat – Daging	
		12:30		Doa Makan			P. Wilem Tulak	
KAMIS	11 MEI	09:00	Mantunu		Potong sisa kerbau		Sie Adat – Daging	
		12:30		Doa Makan			P. Marinus Tellu	
JUMAT	12 MEI	08:00	Mea / pemakaman					
		10:00		Misa Requiem			Pastor Paroki	
		12:00	Mea					
		13:00			Istirahat		Keluarga	

Genealogies of the Gods

GENEALOGY OF THE GODS NO. 1

PUANG MATUA
SEPARATED HEAVEN AND EARTH
AND CREATED THREE DESCENDANTS

PONG BANGGAI RANTE
(VAST PLAIN)

GAUN TIKEMBONG
(EXPANDING CLOUD)

PONG TULAK PADANG
(SUPPORTER OF THE EARTH)

(1)

USUK SANGBAMBAN
(ONE RIB)

ARANG DI BATU
(RADIANCE IN THE ROCK)

(2)

BONGGA LANGI'NA

DATU LAUKKU'

THEIR OFFSPRING LIVED
IN HEAVEN FOR SIX GENERATIONS

BURA LANGI'
THE FIRST MAN TO DESCEND UPON EARTH

KEMBONG BURA

PONG MULA TAU
THE FIRST MAN TO BE BORN ON EARTH

SANDA BILIK

LONDONG DI LANGI'   **TUMBA' ANGGA TANA**   **LONDONG DI RURA**

TANGDILINO
DESCENDANT OF THE
SIXTH GENERATION

BUEN MANIK

(1) GAUN TIKEMBONG CREATED USUK SANGBAMBAN OUT OF HIS RIB

(2) USUK SANGBAMBAN CREATED FIRST HUMAN (WOMAN) DATU LAUKKU'

7 DESCENDANTS

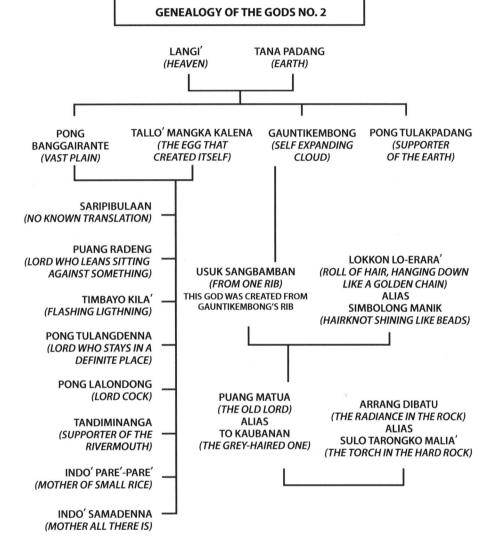

GENEALOGY OF THE GODS NO. 2

LANGI'
(HEAVEN)

TANA PADANG
(EARTH)

PONG
BANGGAIRANTE
(VAST PLAIN)

TALLO' MANGKA KALENA
(THE EGG THAT
CREATED ITSELF)

GAUNTIKEMBONG
(SELF EXPANDING
CLOUD)

PONG TULAKPADANG
(SUPPORTER
OF THE EARTH)

SARIPIBULAAN
(NO KNOWN TRANSLATION)

PUANG RADENG
(LORD WHO LEANS SITTING
AGAINST SOMETHING)

TIMBAYO KILA'
(FLASHING LIGTHNING)

PONG TULANGDENNA
(LORD WHO STAYS IN A
DEFINITE PLACE)

PONG LALONDONG
(LORD COCK)

TANDIMINANGA
(SUPPORTER OF THE
RIVERMOUTH)

INDO' PARE'-PARE'
(MOTHER OF SMALL RICE)

INDO' SAMADENNA
(MOTHER ALL THERE IS)

USUK SANGBAMBAN
(FROM ONE RIB)
THIS GOD WAS CREATED FROM
GAUNTIKEMBONG'S RIB

LOKKON LO-ERARA'
(ROLL OF HAIR, HANGING DOWN
LIKE A GOLDEN CHAIN)
ALIAS
SIMBOLONG MANIK
(HAIRKNOT SHINING LIKE BEADS)

PUANG MATUA
(THE OLD LORD)
ALIAS
TO KAUBANAN
(THE GREY-HAIRED ONE)

ARRANG DIBATU
(THE RADIANCE IN THE ROCK)
ALIAS
SULO TARONGKO MALIA'
(THE TORCH IN THE HARD ROCK)

GENEALOGY OF THE GODS NO. 3

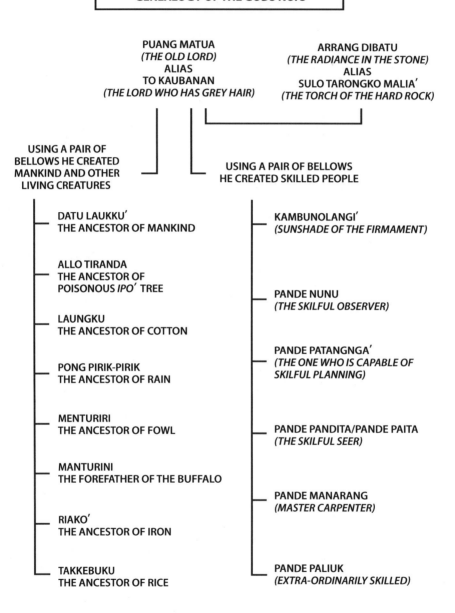

PUANG MATUA
(THE OLD LORD)
ALIAS
TO KAUBANAN
(THE LORD WHO HAS GREY HAIR)

ARRANG DIBATU
(THE RADIANCE IN THE STONE)
ALIAS
SULO TARONGKO MALIA'
(THE TORCH OF THE HARD ROCK)

USING A PAIR OF BELLOWS HE CREATED MANKIND AND OTHER LIVING CREATURES

USING A PAIR OF BELLOWS HE CREATED SKILLED PEOPLE

DATU LAUKKU'
THE ANCESTOR OF MANKIND

ALLO TIRANDA
THE ANCESTOR OF POISONOUS *IPO'* TREE

LAUNGKU
THE ANCESTOR OF COTTON

PONG PIRIK-PIRIK
THE ANCESTOR OF RAIN

MENTURIRI
THE ANCESTOR OF FOWL

MANTURINI
THE FOREFATHER OF THE BUFFALO

RIAKO'
THE ANCESTOR OF IRON

TAKKEBUKU
THE ANCESTOR OF RICE

KAMBUNOLANGI'
(SUNSHADE OF THE FIRMAMENT)

PANDE NUNU
(THE SKILFUL OBSERVER)

PANDE PATANGNGA'
(THE ONE WHO IS CAPABLE OF SKILFUL PLANNING)

PANDE PANDITA/PANDE PAITA
(THE SKILFUL SEER)

PANDE MANARANG
(MASTER CARPENTER)

PANDE PALIUK
(EXTRA-ORDINARILY SKILLED)

Glossary and Index

harvest and the welfare of the community 37, 46–47, 49, 61, 72, 79

Bugis 17, 26–29, 33–35, 37, 110

bupati (Ind.) – high-ranking official, chief of the administrative unit *kabupaten* 60–61

Calvinist Mission Alliance 38, 51, 53, 70

coffee war 34

conversion 15, 20, 55–56, 102, 118

Crystal, Eric 20

Dammen, Stanislaus A. 91–94, 97, 99

dapo' (Tor.) – kitchen 66

Dayak 25, 65

deata (Tor.) – deity 37, 41, 47, 61, 77, 79, 89, 119

Deutero-Malay 26, 65

dipalimang bongi (Tor.) – funeral ritual lasting five days 62

dipapitung bongi (Tor.) – funeral ritual lasting seven days 63

dipasang bongi (Tor.) – funeral ritual lasting one day 62

dipatallung bongi (Tor.) – funeral ritual lasting three days 62

disilli' (Tor.) – funeral ritual performed for the death of an infant 62

Dong Son 25–26

Duri 34

erong (Tor.) – hanging grave 69

Eykemans, Chris 54

Father John – see Manta', John

Father Lucas – see Paliling, Lucas

Father Stanis – see Dammen, Stanislaus A.

Gajah Mada 18, 65

gambling 33, 59, 89

gayang (Tor.) – traditional Toraja dagger 33, 81

gembala (Ind.) – shepherd 71

geography 16, 25, 29, 39

Gereformeerde Zendings Bond – see Calvinist Mission Alliance

grave 68–69, 109

head-hunting 62

Islam 15, 17, 32–33, 53, 61, 79, 108–117, 121

issong (Tor.) – wooden trough used for the threshing of rice 94, 99

Java 18, 26, 30–31, 33, 46, 71, 84, 86, 105, 112

kabongo' (Tor.) – wooden sculpture representing the head of a buffalo, life size 67, 72

kabupaten (Ind.) – territorial administrative unit consisting of kecamatans 29–30, 60

Kalimantan 30, 32, 65, 84, 86

kandaure (Tor.) – adornment made of tiny coloured beads; worn on ceremonial occasions by women on the upper part of their body; it can also be placed on a bamboo canopy to decorate a structure which resembles a half-open umbrella 64, 81, 90, 111

katia (Tor.) – funeral dance performed to welcome the guests 90, 96

katik (Tor.) – statue of a bird with a long neck, with a head similar to a hen's; as a rule it is placed on the house 67

Kaudern, Walter 27

kebaya (Ind.) – blouse-like article of women's clothing 70

kecamatan (Ind.) – territorial administrative unit; several *kecamatan* compose a *kabupaten* 30

Kennedy, Raymond 27

Kruyt, Albert C. 26–28

ladang (Ind.) – non-irrigated field 30

lakkian (Tor.) – wooden tower upon which the coffin is placed for the duration of several days at aristocratic funerals 86, 88, 92 96–98

lamba-lamba (Tor.) – red fabric, under which the family of the deceased nobleman walk during the funeral procession 95, 97

liang (Tor.) – burial vault of rock 68–69

Luwu' (kingdom) 28–29, 33–34

ma'bugi (Tor.) – ritual of purification 47

Ma'dika (Tor.) – aristocratic title 46, 60

ma'lambuk (Tor.) – threshing grains of rice 94–95

ma'pasilaga tedong (Tor.) – buffalo fights 72, 74

ma'popendeme' (Tor.) – throwing meat from the bala'kaan tower at aristocratic funerals 88

ma'tallang (Tor.) – system of division of inheritance according to the number of buffaloes the respective heirs sacrificed at the funeral 93

Majapahit 65

Makale 30–31, 36–37, 47, 51, 53–54, 60, 109

malam empat puluh (Ind.) – ceremony of the Fortieth Night, performed by Toraja Muslims as one of the ceremonies following the burial of the deceased 109–110

mana' (Tor.) – family property that must not be sold 64

Manta', John 73, 88, 93, 95–96, 99

maro (Tor.) – ritual of purification 45, 47, 61

[1] Typical Toraja village with houses on one side and granaries on the other (Ke'te' Kesu')

[2] *Simbuang* stelae (Bori)

[3] Traditional Toraja house (Lembang Tallung Penanian)

[4] *Liang* rock tombs (Lo'ko' Mata)

[5] Remains of the *erong* – hanging graves (Ke'te' Kesu')

[6] *Liang* rock tombs featuring *tau-tau* statuettes (Lemo) | Photo: Martin Točík

[7] *Tau-tau* statuettes (Lemo) | Photo: Martin Točík

[8] Preparation of the *pesung* offerings (Randan Batu)

[9] *Pesung* offerings (Mandetek)

[10] Young dancers in traditional attire (Ke'te' Kesu')

[11] *Katia* dancers and singers (To' Pao)

[12] Catholic Priest John Manta' at a funeral (To' Pao)

[13] Erecting the *simbuang* stele (To' Pao)

[14] Sacrificed buffaloes (To' Pao)

[15] Carving up the meat (To' Pao)

[16] Horns of the sacrificed buffaloes (Ke'te' Kesu')

[17] *Bala'kaan* – tower from which the meat is distributed (To' Pao)

[18] Boys catching portions of meat thrown from the *bala'kaan* (To' Pao)

[19] Ceremonial platform (To' Pao)

[20] Procession of the bereaved under the red fabric – *lamba-lamba* (To' Pao)

[21] Preparations for the transfer of the coffin to the *lakkian* tower (To' Pao)

[22] *Pradula* sarcophagus (Sangalla')

[23] Old woman at a funeral (Ke'te' Kesu')

[24] Small boy in a rice field (near Rembon)

[25] My main informant Tato' Dena' with the *pesung* offering (Mandetek)

[26] Catholic Priest Lucas Paliling (Lili' Kira') | Photo: Martin Točík

[27] Catholic Priest Stanislaus Dammen (To' Pao)

[28] *Kandaure* and *ambero* (worn around the waist) ornaments | Photo: Stanislaus Dammen

Michaela Budiman

Contemporary Funeral Rituals of Sa'dan Toraja

From Aluk Todolo
to "New" Religions

Published by Charles University in Prague, Karolinum Press
Ovocný trh 3–5, 116 36 Prague 1, Czech Republic
http://cupress.cuni.cz
Prague 2013
Editor Vice-rector Prof. PhDr. Ivan Jakubec, CSc.
Edited by Petra Bílková
Layout by Jan Šerých
Typeset by DTP Karolinum
Printed by Karolinum Press
First edition

ISBN 978-80-246-2228-6